SURVIVAL
KIT
FOR
OVERSEAS
LIVING

SURVIVAL KIT FOR OVERSEAS LIVING

For Americans planning to live and work abroad.

SECOND EDITION

L. Robert Kohls
With an Introduction by David S. Hoopes

INTERCULTURAL PRESS, INC.

Published by Intercultural Press, Inc.
P.O. Box 768
Yarmouth, Maine 04096

© 1984 by L. Robert Kohls
Library of Congress Catalogue Card Number 79-65061
ISBN 0-933662-59-9

Printed in the United States of America

Contents

79813

APPENDICES

To Norma,
my lifelong partner
in the exploration
and mastery
of strange lands
and alien ways.

Preface

Every book is written by many people, and this one is no exception. While they do not share the title page, their imprint appears stamped clearly everywhere in the book. Without them it would never have been produced.

Specifically, David Hoopes went through the manuscript page-by-page, word-by-word, and rewrote sizeable portions of it. Chapters 9–12, 15 and 17 were David's original conception and they add considerably to the overall value of the book.

I asked Franchon Silberstein to provide the initial draft for the postscript on re-entry as this is one of her areas of specialization.

Danielle Rome got behind the project and supported it . . . financially and spiritually. She was also of immeasurable help in making sure that all the work was done properly and on time.

Peggy Pusch capably managed a thousand and one details and labored with great care and skill as editor.

George Renwick critiqued the first draft with insight, pointing out what worked and what did not. Alex Patico did a similar "fine-toothed" analysis.

Serge Ogranovitch, Thomas Walker and Jack Cook served as sounding boards and made many valuable suggestions.

To all, my heartiest thanks.

Robert Kohls

Introduction

I am very pleased to have been associated with the production of this book. For years specialists in the cross-cultural field have sat around bemoaning the fact that a book like this did not exist. Yet none did anything about it. I often wondered why, until I got hold of Bob Kohls' manuscript. It then became clear that none of us had been able to overcome the jargon of our profession or break out of the prison of our academic training. No one was able to write a book that was both substantive in content, yet couched in the language of the layman.

Bob Kohls has done it.

Kohls has been in international and intercultural training for a long time. He's had experience in business, education and government. As Director of Training and Development for the United States Information Agency, his daily job was to convince his colleagues that there was more to be known about functioning abroad than they thought. Later, at the Washington International Center, he had the chance to apply his ideas to orientation programs for foreign students and visitors in the U.S.

There's an air of the author's knowing what he's about in this book. He has a flair for capturing the right idea in the right language, for making the critical points stand out, for taking you step-by-step into the intriguing heart of a sometimes baffling, sometimes frustrating, but almost always immensely rewarding experience.

But he doesn't do it ploddingly, exhausting the reader and the subject in the process. Instead, he moves you through the book at high speed, stopping to ask you questions and get you to probe your own thoughts and feelings, but then taking you on a lively pace to examine each successive stage of the overseas experience. It is therefore a book you will get through quickly, but one you'll be thinking about for a long, long time.

David S. Hoopes

SURVIVAL KIT FOR OVERSEAS LIVING

So you're going overseas

It's been decided. You're going to accept the opportunity to spend some time working and living in another country. Now you're getting ready, doing the thousand and one things necessary to get yourself and, perhaps, your family launched. Or maybe you're already on the plane, seat back reclined, legs stretched out, finally able to relax for a moment and let your mind wander.

You've probably had too little time to think seriously about what's ahead, what it's going to be like living in a "foreign" country. There are very few sources of good information about overseas living and the perspective of those who've gone before you is skewed by their own particular experiences and how they've perceived them.

Yet, unless you've spent a long time in a foreign country already, there are unanticipated surprises in store. The success rate of overseas adjustment among Americans is not nearly as high as it might be. If left to luck, your chances of having a really satisfying experience living abroad would be about one in seven.

But it doesn't have to be left to luck. There are things you can do. Specifically, you and your family can give some organized thought to *planning* and *preparing* for the experience. Many people devote most of their energy to the logistics of getting launched and, in fact, *do* leave the rest to luck. The wiser person looks further ahead. There may be many unknowns or uncertainties but it's possible to lay the groundwork for a productive time overseas. The purpose of this book is to show how it can be done.

Curiously, what people need most when they go overseas is to understand themselves better as Americans—because when they go they will carry with them all the ''cultural baggage'' they have accumulated during their lifetimes. One of the purposes of this book is to help you become aware of your cultural baggage and suggest ways in which to avoid tripping over it too often.. To do so we need to ask what is it in the American environment that has made you what you are and how can an awareness of your *Americanness* provide the basis for understanding and coping effectively with your experiences in a foreign country?

Over there, the environment and the culture have been busy shaping people into Frenchmen, Japanese, Arabs, Chinese, Colombians, or whatever. The question is how can you as an American direct your efforts toward learning, in the quickest, most cost-effective manner, about how to function at your optimum capacity in the non-American environment into which you are soon to be, quite literally, dropped?

The material presented in these pages is designed to provide the answer to those questions. The ideas are stated as succinctly as possible and yet attempt to get at some of the deeper issues which are central to functioning effectively overseas.

The book doesn't preach. More often than not you will be asked to think through the issues on your own in brief structured exercises. The book should be seen as a resource for getting you into and through an experience which, like white water rafting, is exciting and rewarding, but which has its shoals and rapids. It's a book you can come back to when the going gets rough. It's a SURVIVAL KIT FOR OVERSEAS LIVING.

2

Others have gone before

You're not the first American to leave our shores to try your hand at living in another country. Thousands have gone before and set the stage for your arrival . . .

Yes, your way has been paved—with bad impressions!

All over the world people think they know all about Americans. They've watched American tourists, American films, and American TV programs. Their radios and newspapers have blared forth sensational news about the United States. They've heard incredible stories from countrymen who have visited the U.S.

The result has been, at best, an incomplete view of what Americans are like; at worst, a distorted one. Out of this incomplete or distorted information have emerged stereotypes—fixed, simplified impressions of what Americans are. Stereotypes are natural; they are one way people everywhere deal with things which are too complex to handle or about which they have inadequate information.

But they are also destructive in personal encounters because they are unfair and because they interfere with getting to know people.

You will be confronted often with stereotypes. People will judge you not on the basis of who you are and the signals you give off, but on the stereotypes they have formed long before they knew you existed.

How will you respond? What kind of stereotypes do you think you will encounter? Take a moment before turning the page to jot down in

Duane Hanson sculpture, *Tourists* (1970), photographed by Eric Pollitzer.

the space provided some of the stereotypes of Americans you think are most commonly held abroad.

Then go on and see how they compare with our list.

3

The stereotyped American

Here are some of the most common stereotypes of Americans held by people in other countries.

Americans are:

- ✓ OUTGOING, FRIENDLY
- ✓ INFORMAL
- LOUD, RUDE, BOASTFUL, IMMATURE
- ✓ HARD WORKING
- EXTRAVAGANT, WASTEFUL
- CONFIDENT THEY HAVE ALL THE ANSWERS
- ✓ LACKING IN CLASS CONSCIOUSNESS
- DISRESPECTFUL OF AUTHORITY
- RACIALLY PREJUDICED
- IGNORANT OF OTHER COUNTRIES
- ✓ WEALTHY
- ✓ GENEROUS
- ALWAYS IN A HURRY

It is also widely believed that:

- ALL AMERICAN WOMEN ARE PROMISCUOUS

How many of the listed items are positive and how many are negative? Go through and put a check beside the positive ones and underline the negative ones.

Most of us would probably consider five or six of the fourteen points to be positive. To Americans, "outgoing, friendly" and "lacking in class consciousness," to mention only a couple, are considered to be virtues. Yet, the reserved Britisher who finds his seatmate on a transatlantic flight an outgoing, back-slapping American may have quite a different opinion. Someone from a country with a very structured, hierarchical social system, such as India, may consider our lack of class consciousness an affront.

The point is that what we think are positive values or admirable characteristics may not be considered so by others. What we believe to be a positive stereotype may, in fact, be a negative one in the eyes of a person from another country.

Which brings us to a fundamental point: that throughout the world there are many different ways of doing things, most of which are *intrinsically* neither better nor worse than our own. They are simply different.

Stereotypes are not always wrong. Some of them contain too much truth for comfort. The problem with stereotypes, really, is that they prevent us from getting to the richer reality which lies beyond them.

One thing is sure: At some point when you are overseas, you will encounter these stereotypes and there will be those who will hold you *personally* responsible for them. It's very likely you will be called upon to answer some very pointed questions based on them.

When we asked you above about how you would respond to being stereotyped, what were your thoughts? If someone says to you: "Why are Americans such racists? such imperialists? so rude? so rushed all the time?" what will you say in reply?

There are no pat answers, of course. Each person must form his or her own unique responses. Experience has shown, however, that the following are useful guidelines:

1. Resist becoming angry or defensive
2. Avoid fitting the stereotype
3. Persist in being your (sweet old) self

If your sweet old self fits one of the stereotypes, then you've got a problem. Better in the beginning to avoid the stereotype and to let your real personality emerge as you become more comfortable in the environment.

Indeed, anything you can do to help break the negative stereotypes people have of Americans will contribute 1) to your own pleasure in the overseas experience, 2) to the pleasure of those who follow you, 3) to the improvement of the American image abroad, and 4) even perhaps a smidgeon to world understanding. Quite a collection of accomplishments for so small an effort.

Now let's look at the other side of the stereotyping coin. All over the world there are friendly, hospitable people ready and eager to welcome Americans into their societies.

What kinds of attitudes do we as a group have about them and their cultures? Are we ever guilty of a little counterproductive stereotyping of our own?

4

The ugly American

The novel *The Ugly American*[1] struck the Americans of the late 1950's like a thunderbolt. It came at a time when the nation was moving internationally into high gear. Americans were swarming about the world as never before. Tourists, diplomats, students, scholars, technical experts, businessmen, military advisors, were spreading around the world an image of Americans which came to be embodied in many of the negative stereotypes discussed in the previous chapter. *The Ugly American* held a mirror up before us, and it was with a distinct shock that we recognized the reflection we saw. We were embarrassed by the behaviors and attitudes Americans displayed as guests in other countries.

To a significant extent because of *The Ugly American,* we are much more conscious today of our behavior overseas, particularly in our words and deeds. We still carry with us, however, a number of deeply inbedded attitudes which tap into our darker nature and emerge from time to time in our international contacts.

Following is a list of some of those attitudes. A number are quite commonly held and may not, at first glance, seem offensive. Others are to be found only in the extremely narrow-minded or, indeed, in the bigot. Look the list over and check those which reflect what you feel is a defensible position.

1. By Eugene Burdick and William Lederer (New York: Norton, 1958). Ironically, the "Ugly American" in the book was in reality the good guy, who was sensitive to other cultures. The term was soon turned around, however, to refer to the loud, insensitive, exploitative brand of overseas Americans.

1. The fact that America was able to place a man on the moon proves America's technological superiority.

2. Foreigners coming to live in the U.S. should give up their foreign ways and adapt to America as quickly as possible.

3. Orientals do many things backwards.

4. Much of the world's population remains "under-developed" because they don't take the initiative to develop themselves.

5. English should be accepted as the universal language of the world.

6. The Vietnamese and other Southwest Asians do not place value on human life; to them life is cheap.

7. Americans have been very generous in teaching other people how to do things the right way.

8. Minority members of a population should conform to the customs and values of the majority.

9. If everyone learned to do things the way we do, the world would be better off and people everywhere would understand each other better.

10. Primitive people have not yet reached the higher stages of civilization.

Can you convert these into objective statements? For instance, No. 1: "By placing a man on the moon, America demonstrated the great emphasis which it as a society places on technological development." Consider the others.

More important—as they stand, what central theme runs through all of these statements?

Look them over again carefully before reading on.

State the central theme briefly in the space below.

˙ The theme as *we* see it is: the explicit or implicit assumption of the superiority of one group over another, humankind's ancient ethnocentric[2] impulse. We all believe in our heart of hearts that *our* race, *our* culture, *our* group is the most important, worthy, civilized, etc., in the world. It's a primordial instinct which from the beginning of the species has served a basic survival function by linking us to and strengthening the group from which we derive our security, thus assuring the group's continuance.

Unfortunately it is also a destructive impulse from which war, hate, oppression, and prejudice flow. There is little hope of ever being wholly freed from it because it is a largely subconscious impulse and influences our attitudes and behaviors without our being aware of it.

But there are things we can do to manage and control our ethnocentrism, and we will examine them one-by-one in the chapters which follow.

First, however, let's take a closer look at one of the attitudes which crops up all too often as a stumbling block to effectiveness overseas.

---

2. Webster's definition of ethnocentrism is: "regarding one's own race or cultural group as superior to others."

5

Primitivism reconsidered

"Primitive people have not yet reached the higher stages of civilization."

For anyone involved in international activities this is an especially insidious belief.

All of us, by virtue of our enculturation[3] in Western society in general, and in American society in particular, have deeply imbedded within us certain ideas regarding what it means to be "civilized" and what it means to be "primitive."

Think, for a moment, of the dictionary definition of the words "civilization" and "civilized."

We have been taught that "civilization" represents an advanced state of human development, with an extremely high level of achievement and sophistication in the arts, and sciences, technology, government, and social institutions. (To us, even our religion has long since moved out of the morass of superstition and magic.)

"Primitive," on the other hand, denotes a state of simplicity bordering on ignorance, or at least on the simplicity of the untutored child. That which is primitive is rudimentary, unsophisticated, and superstitious. Primitive peoples, according to the common definition, are closer to the state of our primordial ancestors who wandered the forests on all fours looking for food and shelter.

---

3. Enculturation is an anthropological term which refers to the process of being trained in the values and behaviors of one's parent society.

The picture we carry in our minds looks something like this·

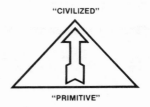

Of course, *we're* the ones who are civilized.

This idea flowered in 19th-century Europe when, under the influence of Darwin, theorists attempted to apply the idea of evolution to the development of society as a whole. One of the results was that 19th-century Europeans saw themselves as the end product and at the apex of human civilization.

This kind of thinking was graphically epitomized by Lewis Morgan, a well-known 19th century anthropologist, in his "Pyramid of Human Development."

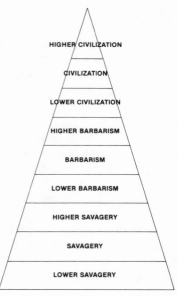

Lewis Morgan's "Pyramid of Human Development"

To accompany the Pyramid, Morgan developed clear and precise definitions for each stage, from "lower savagery" to "higher civilization," and then classified every known group of people within one of the stages.

This once respected work now seems ludicrous. It would no longer be accepted by respected anthropologists anywhere (that in itself is a sign we've made some advances in cultural awareness!).

We know now that most societies once called primitive are in fact highly developed civilizations with complex and sophisticated social structures and cultural patterns, each with its own peak achievements. They have been judged too often, however, on their failure to encompass the technological and scientific accomplishments of the West.

But Morgan's basic ideas linger on in our present attitudes toward non-Western peoples, even though many of us have long since learned that it is not "nice" to refer to a specific country or its people as "primitive," at least not to their faces.

Actually, we've made honest attempts to find an acceptable term to describe the differences which clearly exist between industrial and non-industrial nations, having over the years gone from one term to the next.

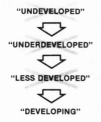

"UNDEVELOPED"

"UNDERDEVELOPED"

"LESS DEVELOPED"

"DEVELOPING"

Yet, in the end, they have all proved equally insulting because Lewis Morgan and his Pyramid still lurk within us.

The term "third world," while originally political in meaning, seems to be gaining favor as the least derogatory way of referring to the societies once identified as "primitive." At least this term does the country the courtesy of assuming that it is involved in intentional movement in a direction of its own. "Traditional" is also sometimes acceptable where modern industrial and technological development have not yet had a strong impact.

Another thing we can do to neutralize the effect of Morgan's ideas is to compare cultures on a co-equal basis, as in the diagram below. If we call the two cultures "X-culture" (instead of "civilized") and "Z-culture" (instead of "primitive") we can show them without making assumptions of superiority:

Any areas of commonly held values which exist, and there are usually many, may be diagrammed in this way:

This takes us back now to our earlier question: How do you go about bringing your ethnocentrism under control?

The answer: You bring it to the surface, look at it, and shift the emphasis from cultural inferiority and superiority to cultural similarities and differences—as we have done with our "X" and "Z" cultures.

Another useful undertaking is to become acquainted with the nature of "culture" itself.

6

Culture defined

The word "culture" has literally dozens of definitions—most of which will be ignored here. By culture, for instance, we do *not* mean the intellectually and socially "cultured" person, nor do we refer to the arts—literature, painting, the opera, etc. These are valid meanings of the word, but not what is being referred to here.

Instead, we are using "culture" in the anthropological sense. For the purposes of this book here is the definition we like best:

CULTURE = an *integrated system* of *learned behavior patterns* that are characteristic of the members of any given society. Culture refers to the *total way of life* of particular groups of people. It includes everything that a group of people *thinks, says, does,* and *makes*—its *systems of attitudes and feelings*. Culture is *learned* and *transmitted* from generation to generation.

By this definition, we can see that a particular culture would consist of at least the following:

- Manners
- Customs
- Beliefs
- Ceremonies
- Rituals

- Social institutions
- Religious beliefs
- Myths and legends
- Knowledge
- Values

- Laws (written and unwritten)
- Ideas and thought patterns
- Language
- Arts and artifacts
- Tools

- Concept of self
- Morals
- Ideals
- Accepted ways of behaving

In short, culture is the *total way of life* of any group of people.

It is obvious, therefore, that culture is woven intricately into the very fiber of every member of the group and is one of the controlling influences in the way people live—the way they think, the way they speak, and the way they behave. When these "patterns of culture," which are built into each of us, encounter other and different patterns of culture (as occurs when you go from your own culture group to live in another, for example), conflict, dissonance, and disorientation are the almost inevitable result.

"Culture," thus, is central to the experience of living overseas. The next several chapters will be spent delving rather deeply into what culture is and how it affects you as an American.

Now that we have a working definition of culture, we're ready to make a number of generalizations which follow naturally one from the other:

1. By definition, to be "human" means to be part of a culture. It is impossible to conceive of humans outside of culture. Humans create culture and culture creates humans.

2. Most cultures developed separately, in isolation, thousands of years ago. The ways which eventually developed were adapted and evolved slowly and painstakingly, through trial and error, by each group independently. The course of this evolution was based primarily on the ability of each element in the culture to contribute to the physical and psychological survival of the group.

3. The culture of any group represents an extremely complex and interrelated package where every aspect is interwoven and intermeshed with all other aspects. To change any one part of a culture inevitably affects many other parts of the culture.

4. Every society, in developing its own culture, must meet the needs of the group in at least ten basic areas. The first three items on the following list are generally recognized as the "necessities of life." This

is true if we are thinking of individuals. If we speak of society as a whole, however, the last seven items may be seen as equally "necessary" to maintain culture.

- Food
- Clothing
- Shelter
- Family organization
- Social organization
- Government
- Defense
- Arts/Crafts
- Knowledge/Science
- Religion

5. It was highly likely, indeed almost inevitable, that different groups would come up with different sets of solutions to these ten basic needs.

6. There are no intrinsically "right" or "wrong" solutions, no objectively provable "better" or "worse" ways of meeting these needs. There are not absolutes. For practical purposes, there are only *different* solutions. This is a key point and a very complex issue. We are not advocating ethical or moral neutrality. Approval of such practices as head shrinking, human sacrifice or cannibalism is not required or even recommended in order to recognize that there is an *inherent logic* in every culture. To understand different values and behaviors, it is useful to approach them non-judgmentally, searching for that which in inherently logical rather than automatically either condemning or accepting them.

7. An equally key point is that every group of people, every culture, is, and has always been, ethnocentric; that is, it thinks its own solutions are superior and would be recognized as superior by any right-thinking, intelligent, logical human being. It is significant that to each group, their own view of the world appears to be the "common sense" or "natural" view. Let's take a brief look, by the way of example, at Americans and the cultural characteristic of *cleanliness*. We generally consider ourselves among the cleanest people in the world. We're quick to criticize many other countries and cultures as being "dirty." Yet consider for a moment the following:

- When Americans bathe, they soak, wash and rinse their bodies in the same water—though they would never wash their clothes and dishes that way. The Japanese, who use different water for each of these steps, find the American way of bathing hard to understand, even dirty.

- An orthodox Hindu from India considers it "dirty" to eat with knives, forks, and spoons instead of with his own clean fingers.

- Is it dirtier to spit and blow your nose on the street or to carry it around with you in a little piece of cloth which you keep in your pocket and re-use regularly?

- Many people around the world cannot understand why Americans invariably defecate in the same room where they wash and bathe, or why, in so many modern American homes, the toilet is placed so near the kitchen.

8. The process through which the accumulated culture of any group is passed on to its offspring is, as noted above, called "enculturation." Every person is enculturated into a particular culture. One could say that each society enculturates its own offspring into its own "right way" of doing things.

9. People who stay strictly within their own cultures can go on indefinitely without ever having to confront their ethnocentric of enculturated selves.

10. Problems arise, however, when a person who is enculturated into one culture is suddenly dropped into another, very different culture.

It is at this point, as we mentioned earlier, that conflict, dissonance and disorientation set in. The common term for this effect is "culture shock." Anyone entering a new environment to live will experience culture shock in some degree. They will also be offered the opportunity to learn and grow in unique and exciting ways.

We'll talk about culture shock in more detail later.

Right now, in order to provide you a basis for both coping with the overseas experience and exploiting it to the fullest for your own benefit, we need to explore how best to interpret and analyze cultures. What you need are some tools—conceptual tools, in this case—which will enable you to sort out the basic elements of culture and deal with them rationally and systematically.

7

Comparing and contrasting cultures

The husband and wife team of Clyde and Florence Kluckhohn, along with fellow anthropologist Frederick Strodtbeck, have provided us with one of the needed tools. Looking at the phenomenon of culture analytically and philosophically, they came up with five basic questions that get at the root of any culture's value system, no matter how different or seemingly exotic.

1. What is the character of innate human nature? = Human nature orientation
2. What is the relation of Man to Nature? = Man-Nature orientation
3. What is the temporal focus (time sense) of human life? = Time orientation
4. What is the mode of human activity? = Activity orientation
5. What is the mode of human relationships? = Social orientation

Consider for a moment the five orientations in the right-hand column. How would you describe the attitude of the majority of Americans toward each? What do Americans think human beings are like basically? What kind of relationship do they have to nature? What does time mean to them? How important is action? What kind of relationship do they have with each other?

The chart which follows is an adaptation and simplification of one developed by Kluckhohn and Strodtbeck. It indicates the range of possible responses to the five orientations. It is intended to be read horizontally, each horizontal box relating to one of the five orientations listed above.[4]

ORIENTATION	BELIEFS AND BEHAVIORS		
HUMAN NATURE ➤	BASICALLY EVIL	MIXTURE OF GOOD AND EVIL	BASICALLY GOOD
RELATIONSHIP OF MAN ➤ TO NATURE	MAN SUBJUGATED BY NATURE	MAN IN IN HARMONY WITH NATURE	MAN THE MASTER OF NATURE
SENSE OF ➤ TIME	PAST-ORIENTED	PRESENT-ORIENTED	FUTURE ORIENTED
ACTIVITY ➤	BEING (Stress on who you are)	GROWING (Stress on self-development)	DOING (Stress on action)
SOCIAL ➤ RELATIONSHIPS	AUTHORITARIAN	GROUP-ORIENTED	INDIVIDUALISTIC

We recognize that in any culture consisting of a large number of people, the whole range of possible human values and behaviors will probably be found, if only in a few individuals. When we talk of American or French or Chinese values, we mean those which predominate within that group; those which are held by enough of its members to make the values an evident and prominent part of the culture as a whole. Let's take a look at each of the five orientations to determine where a typical middle-class American might be expected to fit.[5]

In respect to HUMAN NATURE, average, middle-class/mainstream Americans are generally optimistic, choosing to believe the best about

4. A full outline of the Kluckhohn model is included in Appendix A.
5. Members of American minority groups would probably find their values diverging in some significant respects from those discussed here. If you are a member of a minority or have a strong ethnic identification, attempt to identify ways in which your values and behavior differ from those indicated here as characteristic of mainstream American culture.

a person until that person proves otherwise. Will Rogers was being very American when he said: "I never met a man I didn't like." We would place average Americans in the right-hand column (basically good) as far as Human Nature Orientation goes. This classification explains the interest Americans have in such activities as prison reform and social rehabilitation. Americans generally believe that in order to bring out the basic goodness in human beings all you have to do is change the negative social conditions in which they exist.

The Kluckhohns, however, placed Americans in the left-hand column (basically evil), citing the Christian belief in original sin. This may have been accurate reading for the 1950's, though we have our doubts. For today it seems thoroughly antiquated. Certainly, whether Americans see human nature as good or evil, it is fair to say they accept it as changeable. Indeed, deep down, Americans in general believe humans and human society are ultimately perfectible—if only enough effort is made in that direction.

In the MAN-NATURE orientation, Americans see a clear separation between man and nature (this would be incomprehensible to many Orientals) and man is clearly held to be in charge. The idea that man can control his own destiny is totally alien to most of the world's cultures. Elsewhere people tend to believe that man is driven and controlled by Fate and can do very little, if anything, to influence it. Americans, on the other hand, have an insatiable drive to subdue, dominate, and control their natural environment.

Concerning orientation toward TIME, Americans are dominated by a belief in progress. We are future-oriented. This implies a strong task or goal orientation. We are very conscious too, that "time is money," and therefore not to be wasted. We have an optimistic faith in the future and what the future will bring. We tend to equate "change" with "improvement" and consider a rapid rate of change as normal.

As for ACTIVITY, Americans are so action-oriented that they cannot even conceive what it would be like to be "being"-oriented. Indeed, we are *hyperactive,* to the degree that one sociologist has described the American as an "Electric Englishman." We believe in keeping busy and productive at all times—even on vacation. The faith of Horatio Alger in the work ethic is very much with us. As a result of this action-orientation, Americans have become very proficient at problem solving and decision making.

Our SOCIAL orientation is toward the importance of the individual and the equality of all people. Friendly, informal, outgoing, and extroverted, Americans scorn rank and authority, even when they are the ones with the rank and authority. American bosses are the only supervisors in the world who would insist on being called by their first names by their subordinates. We find it extremely easy to "make friends," and we think there are unlimited friendships out there just waiting to be made. With a strong sense of individuality, family ties in America are relatively weak, especially when compared to the rest of the world. We have succeeded in reducing the family to its smallest possible unit—the nuclear family.

Look back at the Kluckhohn-Strodtbeck model on page 22. If we take the structure of compartments as shown there and fill in the areas into which the predominant American values fall, we come up with a picture of the American value system that looks like this:

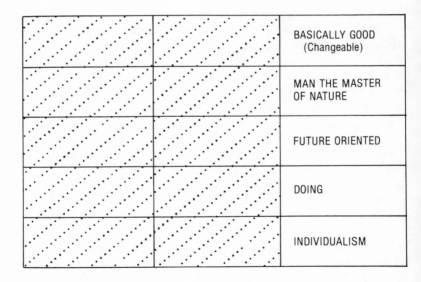

		BASICALLY GOOD (Changeable)
		MAN THE MASTER OF NATURE
		FUTURE ORIENTED
		DOING
		INDIVIDUALISM

Let's look at the value systems of several other societies and compare them with the American.

We recognize that models of this kind are over-simplifications and can only give approximations of reality. Their use is in giving rough pictures of the striking contrasts and differences which may be encountered in societies where certain values predominate, even though they may be in the process of marked change due to rapid modernization. Fundamental values, however, have a way of persisting in spite of change. The evolution of values is a slow process, since they are rooted in survival needs and passed on, almost fanatically, from generation to generation.

We see many of the world's "traditional" cultures as follows:

BASICALLY EVIL		MIXTURE GOOD/EVIL		
	(unchangeable)		(unchangeable)	
MAN SUBJUGATED BY NATURE				
PAST ORIENTED				
BEING				
AUTHORITARIAN				

Here's how we view Arab cultures from a generalized perspective. There would be important variations, of course, from one specific culture to another—Egyptian, Saudi, Lebanese, etc. Notice that in one category—man-nature relationships—the Arabs seem to fall more or less equally into two of the classifications.

	NEUTRAL		
		(unchangeable)	
MAN SUBJUGATED BY NATURE	MAN IN HARMONY WITH NATURE		
PAST ORIENTED			
BEING			
AUTHORITARIAN			

Here's how we see the Japanese (a very complex culture and even more "contradictory" than the Arabs):

	MIXTURE GOOD/EVIL		
		(unchangeable)	
	MAN IN HAR-MONY WITH NATURE		
PAST ORIENTED			FUTURE ORIENTED
	SELF DEVELOPMENT		DOING
AUTHORITARIAN	GROUP ORIENTED		

Interestingly enough, the Hippies during their heyday generally came down the center of the chart, explaining why their values were in such conflict with those of mainstream America.

The Kluckhohn chart only shows three variations out of an infinite variety of possibilities, and it only compares cultures on five basic orientations. It does not claim, therefore, to tell you *everything* about every conceivable culture. Yet it is impressive in the differences in values which it does reveal. In a sense, the values expressed in the right-hand column can be said to be 180° away from the values in the left-hand column.

Is it any wonder that putting Americans into cultures with complex and/or radically different value orientations sometimes causes stress, disorientation, and breakdowns in communication?

In a very simple format, the Kluckhohn chart indicates where the problems are likely to lie.[6] Plot the culture to which you are going in comparison to a middle-class American orientation (or to your own orientation if it varies from the American norm). To do so may call for a little extra reading or a talk with someone who knows the country well.

6. For a study that elaborates on the Kluckhohn model and includes some interesting cross-cultural comparisons see: Edward C. Stewart, *American Cultural Patterns: A Cross-cultural Perspective* (Chicago: Intercultural Press, 1971).

8

What makes
an American?

The use of models, while helpful, tends to be an abstract, academic way of getting at the subject. How can we bring American values, which constitute the core piece of cultural baggage you are taking overseas with you, more sharply into focus?

Have you ever sat down and tried to make a list of American values? Or perhaps "basic ideas held by most Americans"? If you're not an anthropologist or cultural historian it probably won't be easy. But since it's relevant, give it a try.

Write in the space which follows as many American values or basic American ideas as you can think of and, wherever possible, condense them into one- or two-word phrases.

NOTES:

How many did you get? If you have more than ten you're satisfied with, that's good.

There's another way to get at the concrete yet evasive values which guide our lives, a way so simple and integral to the experience of growing up that you may be startled by how easy it is to open a window on what makes us tick as Americans.

In the space below jot down quickly as many proverbs, axioms, and adages as you can dredge up from your memory, Sayings like: "a watched pot never boils," or "a stitch in time saves nine."

How many can you think of?

NOTES:

If your memory is deficient, don't worry. We'll help. But if you did get a list, go back over it before turning this page and write down beside each proverb what *value* you think it is teaching—again in a one- or two-word phrase.

Then go on.

Here is our list, the proverbs on the left and the values they seem to be teaching on the right.

Cleanliness is next to godliness.	CLEANLINESS
A penny saved is a penny earned.	THRIFTINESS
Time is money.	TIME THRIFTINESS
Don't cry over spilt milk.	PRACTICALITY
Waste not; want not.	FRUGALITY

Early to bed, early to rise, makes a man healthy, wealthy, and wise.	DILIGENCE; WORK ETHIC
God helps those who help themselves	INITIATIVE
It's not whether you win or lose, but how you play the game.	GOOD SPORTSMANSHIP
A man's home is his castle.	PRIVACY; VALUE OF PERSONAL PROPERTY
No rest for the wicked.	GUILT; WORK ETHIC
You've made your bed, now sleep in it.	RESPONSIBILITY; RETALIATION
Don't count your chickens before they're hatched.	PRACTICALITY
A bird in the hand is worth two in the bush.	PRACTICALITY
The squeaky wheel gets the grease.	AGGRESSIVENESS
Might makes right.	SUPERIORITY OF PHYSICAL POWER
There's more than one way to skin a cat.	ORIGINALITY, DETERMINATION
A stitch in time saves nine.	TIMELINESS OF ACTION
All that glitters is not gold.	WARINESS
Clothes make the man.	CONCERN FOR PHYSICAL APPEARANCE
If at first you don't succeed, try, try again.	PERSISTENCE; WORK ETHIC
Take care of today and tomorrow will take care of itself.	PREPARATION FOR FUTURE
Laugh and the world laughs with you; weep and you weep alone.	PLEASANT OUTWARD APPEARANCE

Our proverbs list is by no means complete, but we have already enumerated twenty basic American values:

- CLEANLINESS
- THRIFTINESS
- TIME THRIFTINESS
- PRACTICALITY
- FRUGALITY
- DILIGENCE

- RESPONSIBILITY
- AGGRESSIVENESS
- PHYSICAL POWER
- ORIGINALITY
- TIMELINESS OF ACTION
- WARINESS

- INITIATIVE
- GOOD SPORTSMANSHIP
- PRIVACY
- WORK ETHIC

- PHYSICAL APPEARANCE
- PERSISTENCE
- PREPARATION FOR FUTURE
- PLEASANT APPEARANCE

It is evidently much more potent in teaching practicality, for example, to say, "Don't cry over spilt milk" than "You'd better learn to be practical." We have all heard this axiom hundreds of times, and it has made its point.

9

To see ourselves

"O wad some power the giftie gie us to see oursels as others see us!" wrote Robert Burns. Bobby was inspired to this thought by a louse crawling on the bonnet of a lady in the pew in front of him in church, but down through the years we have gotten his point.

What Burns didn't know is that we have had that gift all along but haven't realized it! By lowering our defenses and viewing ourselves through the eyes of people from other cultures—from what is called the "cross-cultural perspective"—we can get a strikingly refreshing view of ourselves. But we have to be ready to accept the reality of what we see, warts (or lice) and all.

We are doomed to carry our complete load of cultural baggage wherever we go. There will be no stripping down to lighten the burden or to make the trip easier. It's important, therefore, to know as much as possible about what our culture has packed for us to carry endlessly about the world.

We believe that every culture has a rough balance between positive and negative aspects. Therefore, to point out the weaker or more negative aspects along with the positive in the process of examining a culture or value system does not constitute an attack on that culture. For me to become more aware of my cultural self in its fullest dimensions is a source of strength because it reinforces my real worth rather than an ethnocentric view of reality. To know ourselves better is to grow.

Let's look at ourselves then from a cross-cultural perspective. Let's listen to some opinions of Americans and American ways held by sensitive, observant, and essentially sympathetic foreign visitors.

In 1835, the Frenchman, Alexis de Toqueville, visited America and on his return to France wrote a book[7] containing such astute observations about the new American Republic that many are as valid today as they were then.

Modern de Toquevilles from many countries still are puzzled and intrigued by the intricacies and enigmas of American culture. Here is a selection of actual observations by recent foreign visitors to this country.[8]

As you read them, take time to ask yourself in each case: 1. Is the observation accurate? and 2. How would you explain the trait in question?

1. Visitor from India:
". . . Americans seem to be in a perpetual hurry. Just watch the way they walk down the street. They never allow themselves the leisure to enjoy life; there are too many things to do . . ."

2. Kenya:
"Americans appear to us rather distant. They are not really as close to other people—even fellow Americans—as Americans overseas tend to portray. It's almost as if an American says, 'I won't let you get too close to me;' it's like building a wall."

3. Turkey:
"Once we were out in a rural area in the middle of nowhere and saw an American come to a stop sign. Though he could see in both directions for miles and no traffic was coming, he still stopped!"

4. Colombia:
"The tendency in the U.S. to think that life is only work hits you in the face. Work seems to be the one type of motivation . . ."

5. Indonesia:
"In the U.S. everything has to be talked about and analyzed. Even the littlest thing has to be 'Why? Why? Why?' I get a headache from such persistent questions."

7. *Democracy in America* is still well worth reading.
8. John P. Feig and John G. Blair, *There is a Difference* (Washington, D.C.: Meridian International House, 1975).

6. Ethiopia:

". . . the American is very explicit; he wants a 'yes' or 'no'. If someone tries to speak figuratively, the American is confused."

7. Iran:

"The first time . . . my (American) professor told me, 'I don't know the answer, I will have to look it up,' I was shocked. I asked myself, 'Why is he teaching me?' In my country a professor would give a wrong answer rather than admit ignorance."

These observations are worth examining carefully. They reveal a great deal about us as Americans. For example, take item No. 7:

Most American professors take their status less seriously than Iranian professors do. They prefer to cultivate informal straightforward relationships with their students, often to the point of accepting virtual equality of status. This may go so far as viewing themselves as learners along with the students.

In Iran, where teachers are venerated, this attitude would not be encountered. Students would lose respect for teachers who behaved as American professors do.

American students, on the other hand, approve of the informal, equal-status behavior of their teachers. Americans in general tend to be somewhat skeptical of experts—though they depend heavily on them in crises. But they expect experts to cultivate an air of modesty. Those who are unafraid to admit their ignorance gain our respect. In much of the rest of the world, however, attitudes toward equality and expertise, formality and informality, are quite different.

Before going on, try your hand at explaining the rest of the modern "de Toquevillisms" listed above.

10

Traveling by objectives

It is common in management circles these days to spend a lot of time discussing and setting objectives. Yet how often do we think about "objectives" in our personal lives?

Indeed, how carefully have you examined the motivations which have lead you to opt for the overseas assignment? It might be useful to stop for a moment and examine them again. They are very important because if you are not clear as to exactly what your goals are in going abroad, you will have no way of knowing whether you have reached them. The result will be confusion, uncertainty and the possible erosion of confidence in your decision to go.

Here's a list of the objectives most common among Americans going abroad to live. Check those that apply to you. Then put an "X" beside those that apply to your spouse if you feel they are different from your own. Have your spouse check the list too.

1. Advancement in job or profession
2. Challenge of the specific assignment overseas
3. Opportunity to make more money
4. Pressure from superiors
5. Desire to expand the experience of the family/children
6. Desire to experience an exotic, foreign place
7. Desire to learn another language and culture

8. Desire to keep up with colleagues and friends who have been overseas

9. Desire to get away from life in the United States

10. Need for a change

11. Desire to get away from something in personal or professional life

12. Hope that the new setting will solve something distressing in personal, professional, or family life

13. Hope that foreign experience will stop the drift, uncertainty or pointlessness in your personal or professional life and give it new direction and meaning

14. Other

You've probably checked a number of motives, and that's okay. Plan to return to this list from time to time while you're abroad to test whether the goals you've identified as yours are being achieved.

For the moment, however, go back over the list carefully once more. Are there motivations on the list (or others inside you) that you were unwilling to recognize? Almost everyone who goes abroad has mixed motives, some of which he or she is not too comfortable with. But if these motives are present within you, they will inevitably influence your experience. It's better to get them out on the table than to suppress them. In the open they can be managed and probably transformed by talking with a close friend, discussing them with your spouse, or even getting the advice of a counselor. As long as you have your needs and goals clearly and honestly stated in your own mind and can establish your expectations realistically, they can do little harm in your life overseas, even if they are less idealistic than you might wish them to be.

11

On becoming
a foreigner

You've often had the experience of encountering foreigners in America. Did any of them ever let down their hair and tell you how uncomfortable they felt being a foreigner? If so, you probably have a sense of what those feelings are. Now the tables are turned. Suddenly, *you're* the foreigner and you'll experience the inevitable discomfort yourself.

It will grow as the apparent similarities between you and your hosts are revealed as relatively superficial and the exotic differences become more and more a factor in your daily personal and professional life.

In your own country, you are surrounded by many things which define and reinforce your identity and role—who you are.

Some are symbols—like our country's flag which expresses our national identity.

Some are the accoutrements of role—a briefcase, carpenter's tools, chalk and eraser, a Brooks Brothers suit among male colleagues also attired in Brooks Brothers suits.

Some are people—the President (of your company or country), certain quintessential Americans, a special friend, the local police officer or cabbie.

Some are family—your immediate family members and the relatives that may stretch from coast to coast.

Some are places you enjoy or love—a favorite restaurant, a quiet park, your office, the den in your home, a place of amusement.

Some are physical landmarks—a building, a street, a monument, a mountain in the distance, an ocean shore or the old homestead.

Although many of these may change—friends grow apart, open fields turn into industrial parks—those changes occur within a context that you understand and are a part of. You belong. The fundamental patterns in your relationships and surroundings are generally familiar and predictable.

Stop for a moment and think of the things in your life which mean the most to you, which mean "home," "culture," "community," and "country." Jot them down in the space below if you wish.

NOTES:

When we go overseas, most of these identity reinforcements are suddenly withdrawn; they are replaced with things which, at first, are all too foreign. But what is really foreign is *you*.

There is an important exception to this rule—if you go *en famille,* you take with you a central piece of home identity. Family members may serve as a core support system for one another in confronting and sharing the excitements, frustrations, problems and rewards of the overseas experience.

Even with your family, however, being a foreigner is a new and, at least for a time, an uncomfortable, even threatening experience. It can produce a persistent sense of insecurity vibrating just below the threshold of consciousness—something like a long-term, low-grade infection, not seriously disruptive but annoyingly debilitating. The best antidote is a strong sense of who you are.

In the next chapter we'll look at a few ways to neutralize the negative impact of being a foreigner.

12

A strategy for strangers

One of Robert Heinlein's science fiction novels has an intriguing title—
Stranger in a Strange Land—which captures the essence of the cultural
experience abroad.

What we're going to offer here is a strategy for a stranger entering
a strange land. If strategies work in business, war, and politics, why
not in your venture overseas?

One of the first things learned in a map-reading class is to orient
the map. "Orienting the map" means to get the north indicator on the
map point true north. The next step is to locate yourself on the map and
make sure you know in which direction you are pointed.

These are good instructions for starting out overseas as well. Get
yourself oriented. Make sure you know where you are and in which direction (physically and psychologically) you're pointed.

But how?

Look ahead for a moment. Visualize yourself recently arrived, the
settling-in process satisfactorily started. In what ways should you attempt
to orient yourself after you are actually in-country? Here are a few suggestions:

1. START with your apartment, home, office—whatever is your spa-
tial center—and work out from there in more or less concentric circles.

    a. What places are in the immediate vicinity, what stores, shops,
       services, offices, etc.?

    b. Who inhabits the places nearby, the poor, rich, middle-class? Are they friendly, hostile or neutral?

    c. Locate English-speakers.

  2. NEXT, explore further into the neighborhood nearby.

    a. Locate restaurants and other places where people gather.

    b. Locate transportation.

    c. Locate government offices—the post office, the police, the schools, administrative offices.

3. BEGIN TO LEARN the basic names and phrases that appear on the signs, the names of foods, or services. Learn to read the street signs. Learn the monetary system.

4. LOOK FOR THE DIFFERENCES. Are needs met differently here from the way they are at home? Are things organized differently? (What's the logic or custom behind the naming of streets?) Are there different combinations of food or other goods in the stores or markets? What goods are displayed most prominently? What does that tell you? What buildings stand out? How do you get a taxi, pay on a bus? There is bound to be something vital to you that seems to be totally missing. Does this society ignore a basic human need? Don't panic. The need is probably met in a different way from what you're used to.

5. TALK TO PEOPLE. Identify friendly English speakers and develop an acquaintanceship. Don't be afraid to ask questions. Most people are very anxious to tell foreigners about their country. Go systematically into the different stores and offices and strike up conversations with anyone who will talk with you. (See the next Chapter "Know Thy Host Country" for subjects to cover.)

6. ACCEPT THE HELP OF OTHER AMERICANS, BUT . . . You will almost certainly encounter other Americans virtually the minute you arrive. You may have friends anxiously awaiting your plane. All to the good. Other Americans can provide you much information quickly. Because of other Americans and friendly host nationals, in fact, your transition into the new society will probably be relatively smooth under any circumstances.

BUT it is important to remember that living in another country stirs up complex emotions and responses. Each person's reactions are very nearly unique. Yours will be too. It is therefore important not to let your perception of your host country be filtered too much through the eyes and experience of other Americans. Accept their help and friendship but be wary of their opinions, especially if they focus excessively on the alleged shortcomings of their hosts. In short, gather information only from Americans who have a basically healthy and positive attitude toward the country and its people. You don't need other people's worn-out prejudices and stereotypes.

13

Know thy host country

Your strategy will, of course, work perfectly. You will soon be settled in. You'll have a whole network of sources of information, or at least willing conversationalists. You'll be partying with friends, exploring fascinating out-of-the-way places and accomplishing great things at the office (if you're the job-holder in the family).

All you have to do now is sit back and enjoy, right?

Wrong.

It just isn't that easy. You have to put much more into it if you're going to get out of your overseas experience what you should. Indeed, as with most things, you will derive from it a value more or less equal to the time, involvement and commitment you put into it. But the effort will be worth it. Learning about a new country on site is a rewarding pursuit.

Of course, you will never feel you know all there is to know about the country. At first you'll feel desperately ignorant. To speed up the process you should consider adopting some sort of plan, like the one suggested below.

Before going on, however, let's consider *where* to gather your information.

BEFORE YOU GO

There are friends and acquaintances who have been there and nationals of the country living in or visiting the U.S. Your city or town may have an international hospitality center through which you can meet foreign visitors. The country's embassy (in Washington) will usually be helpful. Certainly their tourist office (normally in New York) will be. If there is a college or university near you, there is bound to be at least one professor who has studied the country and would be flattered to have his expertise called upon. And there may be a few students from the country who would be willing to talk with you or even visit your home.

AFTER YOU ARRIVE

Of course you'll develop your network and your friends. In addition, there are in most countries all kinds of information available for tourists, some of it quite substantive. If you're in a large city, there will probably be a bookstore stocking books in English—with a good supply covering the host country and culture. Go browse. Look for magazines and newspapers edited in the country but printed in English. If you read the language, of course, a wealth of material will be available to you.

The best means of gathering information from people—whether they be Americans or host nationals—is to ask questions. Talk with people at every chance you get and don't hesitate to ask the questions for which you need answers.

It is disheartening to discover how little really adequate information is available in print about many of the countries and cultures around the world. If your country or destination is among them, take heart. It's more fun and educationally more sound to do it yourself. You'll be discovering what you need to know from the best possible source—the people who are there—and you may even be able to write the guidebook that will help those who follow you.

But that can wait. First you have to collect the information that's useful to you. There are at least nine important information-gathering areas.

1. *History.* Look for something brief unless you're a history nut. Don't get bogged down in a heavy tome that would put an insomniac to sleep.

2. *Basic factual information.* Like natural resources, family organization, religion, art, political structure, etc. Appendix B includes a list of such subject areas.

3. *A human profile.* Develop a profile of an average host national the way we have, in the course of this book, of an average, mainstream American.

For only a handful of countries is a really good profile already prepared and packaged. Yet the profile is the most useful of these devices for getting to know the host country because it contains the "people facts."

You will probably have to experiment to find the best way to make up the profile and it may take quite a while and a lot of digging. One approach is through the grandparent exercise. Assume you are a grandparent in the host country. Then ask yourself what you would tell your grandchildren about the values, behaviors and basic social processes of your country. Suggested topics for this exercise are listed in Appendix C.

4. *Specific do's and don't's for the stranger.* As you know, each culture has its own set of manners, expected behaviors, and unspoken rules. Find out what they are before going or as soon as possible after arriving.

5. *Present-day problems and current national affairs.* This kind of information is necessary to an intelligent understanding of what's going on around you. Learning about current affairs is one of the best ways to get a sense of how people evaluate events from different viewpoints and perspectives. In this process, collect your data and remember to withhold judgment until you're sure you understand what everything means.

6. *Problems you as an American are likely to encounter.* These are problems that are going to arise primarily out of what you bring with you, your "cultural baggage." *Neither you nor the host culture is to blame,* however. You need particularly objective information to begin to solve these problems. Here again, Americans are probably a good source for both the information and the solutions. But beware of emotion-laden biases.

Your best bet will be Americans who are essentially sympathetic to, yet able to be objective about, the country. Don't listen to those who make judgments about the host culture according to its deviation from American standards.

7. *How to meet your logistical needs.* American informants can help here too, though much personal exploration will probably be necessary.

Some resources are listed in Appendix E and a checklist of needed information appears in Appendix D. (This checklist is by no means exhaustive but it will get you started.)

8. *Principal sights, monuments and scenic areas.* There is a high correlation between those foreigners who function at their best overseas and those with the keenest interest in exploring the country to which they are assigned.

A national of the country will probably be your best resource in this venture. Why not invite him or her along as a guide-companion?

9. *Identify the nation's heroes and heroines.* As Americans, we might expect someone who had come to live in the U.S. to know about George Washington or Abraham Lincoln although we probably wouldn't ask. Familiarity with your hosts' myths, history, and famous men and women will endear you to them. This is the kind of ''name-dropping'' nobody minds.

14

Let's play
fifty questions⁹

Here are fifty basic questions about your host country and culture. They are not intended to be an inclusive list. Many more will be suggested as you attempt to answer these. Nevertheless, when you have the answers to the following fifty, you may consider yourself well beyond the beginner stage.

Go through the list now and write down the answers to as many as you can. Return to the list periodically both as a guide and as a check on the progress of your quest for information.

1. How many people who are prominent in the affairs (politics, athletics, religion, the arts, etc.) of your host country can you name?

2. Who are the country's national heroes and heroines?

3. Can you recognize the national anthem?

4. Are other languages spoken besides the dominant language? What are the social and political implications of language usage?

5. What is the predominant religion? Is it a state religion? Have you read any of its sacred writings?

6. What are the most important religious observances and ceremonies? How regularly do people participate in them?

9. Adapted from a list developed by Joan Wilson, Foreign Service Institute, U.S. Department of State. Another guide to what questions to ask when learning about another country and culture "on site" is: Bryan Grey, Ken Darrow, Dan Morrow and Brad Palmquist, *Transcultural Study Guide* (Stanford, CA.: Volunteers in Asia. 1975).

7. How do members of the predominant religion feel about other religions?

8. What are the most common forms of marriage ceremonies and celebrations?

9. What is the attitude toward divorce? extra-marital relations? plural marriage?

10. What is the attitude toward gambling?

11. What is the attitude toward drinking?

12. Is the price asked for merchandise fixed or are customers expected to bargain? How is the bargaining conducted?

13. If, as a customer, you touch or handle merchandise for sale, will the storekeeper think you are knowledgeable, inconsiderate, within your rights, completely outside your rights? Other?

14. How do people organize their daily activities? What is the normal meal schedule? Is there a daytime rest period? What is the customary time for visiting friends?

15. What foods are most popular and how are they prepared?

16. What things are taboo in this society?

17. What is the usual dress for women? for men? Are slacks or shorts worn? If so, on what occasions? Do teenagers wear jeans?

18. Do hairdressers use techniques similar to those used by hairdressers in the United States? How much time do you need to allow for an appointment at the hairdresser?

19. What are the special privileges of age and/or sex?

20. If you are invited to dinner, should you arrive early? on time? late? If late, how late?

21. On what occasions would you present (or accept) gifts from people in the country? What kind of gifts would you exchange?

22. Do some flowers have a particular significance?

23. How do people greet one another? shake hands? embrace or kiss? How do they leave one another? What does any variation from the usual greeting or leave-taking signify?

24. If you are invited to a cocktail party, would you expect to find among the guests: foreign business people? men only? men and women?

local business people? local politicians? national politicians? politicians' spouses? teachers or professors? bankers? doctors? lawyers? intellectuals such as writers, composers, poets, philosophers, religious clerics? members of the host's family? (including in-laws?) movie stars? ambassadors or consular officials from other countries?

25. What are the important holidays? How is each observed?

26. What are the favorite leisure and recreational activities of adults? teenagers?

27. What sports are popular?

28. What kinds of television programs are shown? What social purposes do they serve?

29. What is the normal work schedule? How does it accommodate environmental or other conditions?

30. How will your financial position and living conditions compare with those of the majority of people living in this country?

31. What games do children play? Where do children congregate?

32. How are children disciplined at home?

33. Are children usually present at social occasions? at ceremonial occasions? If they are not present, how are they cared for in the absence of their parents?

34. How does this society observe children's "coming of age?"

35. What kind of local public transportation is available? Do all classes of people use it?

36. Who has the right of way in traffic; vehicles, animals, pedestrians?

37. Is military training compulsory?

38. Are the largest circulation newspapers generally friendly in their attitude toward the United States?

39. What is the history of the relationships between this country and the United States?

40. How many people have emigrated from this country to the United States? Other countries? Are many doing so at present?

41. Are there many American expatriates living in this country?

42. What kinds of options do foreigners have in choosing a place to live?

43. What kind of health services are available? Where are they located?

44. What are the common home remedies for minor ailments? Where can medicines be purchased?
45. Is education free? compulsory?
46. In schools, are children segregated by race? by caste? or class? by sex?
47. What kinds of schools are considered best: public, private, parochial?
48. In schools, how important is learning by rote?
49. How are children disciplined in school?
50. Where are the important universities of the country? If university education is sought abroad, to what countries and universities do students go?

15

Speaking of learning the language

Many people faced with a new assignment overseas vow, in a state of high anticipation, that they'll not only go and explore this far away and exotic land, but that they'll learn the language as well. They will get the books and start tomorrow.

For many that tomorrow never comes. A smattering of phrases is all that results from the abundant good intentions and however many months or years spent abroad.

Many people judge themselves too harshly when they fail to learn the language. The resulting guilt, however, probably does more harm than the failure itself. There are a number of reasons why people don't learn the language of their host country. One is that, for an adult particularly, learning another language from scratch is just plain hard; for some, agony. It takes time, effort, and leaves you open to embarrassment, if not humiliation. It's a forbidding prospect to many people.

What about you? Should you try to learn the language of your new country? That's a question only you can answer, but it's one you should face squarely.

If English is widely used or if your work setting or living environment is an English-speaking one, you can probably manage without the language. But if you're going to countries like Libya or Uruguay or Indonesia, where little English is spoken, it's another matter.

Once you've decided to make the commitment, don't hold back. Put the effort into it that is needed. It will pay off. Also be assured that *anything* you learn will be of value, even if it never comes easy. Words, phrases, fragments of sentences, understood or spoken, open windows on the society, revealing the richness that lies within any culture. It makes the struggle worthwhile. And don't worry about what the host nationals think of your modest or fumbling efforts. Most will be delighted.

Every language has words and phrases that cannot be readily translated, only explained. Such phrases are carriers of culture because they represent special ways a culture has developed to view some aspect of human existence. Through language people classify the world around them. Finding out how one group of people, one culture, makes those classifications is one of the most enjoyable and rewarding aspects of living overseas. It would be sad to miss these through an unwillingness to at least take a stab at learning the language.

A number of books have been written precisely to assist in making the language-learning process more comprehensible and easier to manage. Look them up and spend a few hours browsing.[10] It might change your perspective on the subject.

So to sum up: make a conscious decision early on whether you want to make the commitment to learn to speak the language or not. If you do, then dig in and enjoy it. If you don't, then forget the guilt trip and enjoy learning about the culture in other ways.

10. Two of the best are: Donald N. Larson and William A. Smalley, *Becoming Bilingual: A Guide to Language Learning* (South Pasadena, CA: Practical Anthropology, 1974) and Thomas and Elizabeth Brewster, *Language Acquisition Made Practical: Fields of Methods for Language Learning* (Colorado Springs, CO: Lingua House, 1976).

16

Getting down
to the nitty gritty

Now it's time to get down to the nitty gritty, to ask what it is that really
bothers Americans about living in a foreign country and what it is that
most bothers host nationals about working closely with Americans.

At an institute on intercultural communication held at Stanford
University in 1976, a group of experienced cross-cultural specialists
brainstormed the first question and came up with the following:

- Language barriers
- Lack of mobility
- Indirectness
- Formality, protocol, rank
- The slow pace of life
- Lack of conveniences
- Social customs and expectations
- Alcohol and drug problems
- Family problems
- Health problems
- Emotional instability

Many of these problems are obvious or have been touched upon earlier and need no further comment. Several, however, deserve an addi-
tional word or two.

Lack of mobility

In societies with tighter controls over political activity and movement within the country, Americans often get a feeling of imposed isolation. In some countries there may be severe restrictions on freedom of movement for women or for teenagers. Many non-Western countries have radically different concepts of the way males and females should behave toward each other in public. Frustration may result if basic transportation services are inadequate.

In some instances a psychological immobility may be felt, especially in countries where the freedom to discuss issues openly, to engage in lively political discussions, or to argue your opinions in a friendly way with the nationals is restricted. All of these can have the effect of making an American feel unduly hemmed in.

Indirectness

In some cultures American directness is a source of irritation. In some societies confrontations are avoided at all costs. This can confuse and trouble an outspoken American.

Sense of time and pace of life

For action-oriented Americans it is not easy to adjust to a slower pace. Nor do they appreciate putting up with "red tape," bureaucratic delays, and missed appointments.

Lack of conveniences

These will include many luxuries which you may have come to expect as necessary for the full enjoyment of life: your favorite TV programs and sports events, adequate heating or air conditioning, pure water right from the tap, special foods, modern appliances, etc., etc.

Just remember, it's a trade-off. For everything you are forced to give up, you will be able to discover, if you're open to it, some new dimension of life you have not experienced before. For example, you may have to give up some familiar convenience to work in Brazil, but it will be more than compensated for by the lesson in "loosening up" which Brazil has to teach you.

Alcohol and drug problems

Under the stresses of life in a new environment, some people turn to drink. When it becomes excessive, counseling and closer attention to the psychological impact of the cross-cultural experience are called for. At this point culture shock is transformed from a minor ailment to a major sickness.

The easy availability of drugs and the harsh drug laws in some countries have created explosive situations for teenagers, who are at a vulnerable age anyway.

Most families do well overseas but, given the natural stresses, the family unit can become a tinderbox demanding careful attention to see that the needs of all its members are met.

Family problems

Marital and other family problems which existed prior to departure will rarely improve under the strains of overseas living. Indeed, they will almost certainly get worse. Even the most stable of families can expect new stresses. Solve your marital and family problems before you leave home.

Now to the second question: what is it that most bothers host nationals about working with Americans?

A number of years ago an extensive survey[11] was made of the reactions of foreign nationals to the American experts with whom they worked in their own countries. The responses were revealing and provide a good checklist against which to measure your own behavior abroad.

WHAT BOTHERS FOREIGN COUNTERPARTS ABOUT WORKING WITH AMERICANS

1. They display feelings of superiority; they know the answers to everything.

2. They want to take credit for what is accomplished in *joint* efforts.

3. They are frequently unable or unwilling to respect and adjust to local customs and cultures.

4. They fail to innovate in terms of the needs of the *local* culture.

11. Jack Grey, *The Most Common Criticisms of American Technical Assistants by Their Foreign Co-Workers* (College Station, Texas: Texas A&M, 1957), p. 25.

5. They refuse to work through the normal administrative channels of the country.

6. They tend to lose their democratic ways of working and acting when in a foreign assignment.

It may sound harsh, but it's the way Americans, too often, have been perceived. It's the stuff of stereotypes which only you and others like you can sweep away.

In the months ahead return to this checklist occasionally. Cultural behaviors are so ingrained and so difficult to recognize in ourselves that we need ways of periodically testing whether or not we're still on the right track.

17

The handyman's guide to intercultural communication

We're not trying to develop experts in intercultural communication. It's a hard skill to master completely. Also, it will come to you little by little. By the time you're ready to return home, if you've had your antenna out, you'll be a pretty good handyman or handywoman at communicating across cultures.

What we *can* do is introduce you to some of the processes and alert you to the basic dynamics of intercultural communication.[12]

When you're talking to someone, how often are you aware of the *process* of communication that is taking place?

If you're like most of us, the answer is—virtually never (unless it breaks down!).

Why not?

One reason is that we have been doing it for so long (at least since the doctor slapped us on the rear a few seconds after we were ejected from the womb) and because it seems so simple and natural.

But there's another reason. Communication takes place in the medium of one's culture, which facilitates and reinforces it but also hides it. It's like one of those pictures in children's fun books where figures of animals are buried in a scene and the kids have to find them. Com-

12. The best general book currently available on intercultural communications is: John C. Condon and Fathi Yousef, *An Introduction to Intercultural Communication* (Indianapolis: Bobbs Merrill, 1975).

munication is buried in our own cultural scene and is difficult to extract and look at.

Not so abroad. Communication becomes a major issue. We stumble over it continuously—even if we have learned the language. That's because not only do languages vary from country to country, but so do communication styles and, especially, codes of *non-verbal* communication (more on that in a moment). Also, words don't always translate from one language to another as exactly as we would like.

"Perception" is at the heart of intercultural communication. Down deep, we assume that under normal circumstances we all think about and perceive the world in basically the same way and, therefore, that whatever I say will mean the same to you as it does to me.

Fair assumption?

Of course not.

We misperceive, misinterpret and misunderstand each other all the time, even when we share many values, attitudes, beliefs and ways of doing, being, and thinking.

Doesn't it stand to reason that there are going to be greater possibilities of misperceiving and misunderstanding when in a foreign country?

It does indeed.

Look at the accompanying illustration. Look at it. If there are people with you let them look at it too. Study it for a moment and then go on to the following page.

1. What do you see?
2. If there are others with you, what do they see?
3. Do you and the others see something different?

You probably saw a woman. If you were a young man about town would you be interested in getting a date with her? Did you by any chance see more than one woman? If not, go back and look again. Study the picture carefully. Talk about it with someone else if possible.

Shown in the picture are the heads and shoulders of both an old woman *and* a young woman. But normally you can only see one at a time.

For some people, seeing both women is very difficult.

Which brings us to:

POINT NO. 1.

Our perceptions play tricks on us. Even though we know intellectually that this is true, in our everyday lives we assume an objectivity and a reliability that is not borne out by events. Things are not always as they seem.

Research on responses to this picture has turned up something else interesting: that young people usually see the young woman and older people see the old woman.

Which brings us to:

POINT NO. 2.

We are selective in what we perceive (psychologists call it "selective perception"). In fact, most of what we are seeing, hearing, smelling, tasting or feeling at any moment is screened out by our conscious minds.

We tend to perceive consciously only that which is important to us.

But what, for the most part, determines what it is that we consider important? It is our enculturation, our cultural training.

This culturally-determined perceptual set is the great steamer trunk in the cultural baggage we haul abroad with us.

When the picture of the two women (sometimes called "The Ambiguous Lady") is shown to a *group* of people, those who can't see both women are subject to much good-natured joshing and joking and end up feeling a little stupid.

Which brings us to:

POINT NO. 3.

When you're in a situation (your host culture, for instance) *where everyone perceives something in ways you don't, you feel stupid,* which can be pretty depressing. **Antidote:** get comfortable with feeling a little stupid when you're overseas. It happens to everyone. You'll eventually find out what's going on, and in the meantime you'll save a lot of useless anguish.

Is there anything you can *do* (being a good, action-oriented American) to get yourself ready to charm your hosts abroad with intercultural communication skills?

There certainly is.

Find an acquaintance who is willing to carry on an experimental conversation with you—a neighbor, or an office colleague, or perhaps a stranger on the plane—it shouldn't be a family member or a close friend. Here are the rules of the experiment.

1. Pick a subject of some importance to you (a political issue, juvenile delinquency, stock market investments, sex, taxes, etc.).

2. Discuss it for two minutes without interruption while your partner listens.

3. At the end of the two minutes ask your partner to summarize as accurately as possible what you said.

4. If the summary is inaccurate in *any* way, correct it and ask your partner to re-summarize it.

5. Continue this until your partner has repeated your meaning exactly.

6. Reverse the roles and repeat the exercise.

What does this experiment prove? *Principally* that it is hard to listen well. Too simple? Not at all.

Listening is something of an art. A high percentage of miscommunication occurs because the listener either isn't listening or is listening to the words, not the meaning. The question of effective listening (or "active" listening as it is sometimes called) becomes critical when talking with people from other cultures.

When you are in your own culture there are dozens of little cues which help convey meaning—gestures, facial expressions, body motions ("body language"), eye contact, voice inflections—all of which in the speaker occur automatically and are interpreted immediately by the listener without conscious thought. We've all learned, for example, that "catching the person's eye" is important in some situations. In similar situations abroad, direct eye-contact may be considered impolite or disrespectful. It may, however, be entirely correct in a different context, and *that* may seem strange to you.

Overseas, many, if not most, of these non-verbal methods of elaborating and reinforcing the meaning of a verbal message are different, sometimes very different. Combine this with the fact that the meaning must be interpreted from a different cultural perspective and you have the obvious proposition:

Overseas you have to listen two or three times as hard to people in order to find out what they really mean.

There's another way to help you get at real meanings when you're abroad. This one's basically easy, but will take some courage.

Ask the person you're talking with.

Another oversimplification? We don't think so. If you want the technical term, it's called "perception-checking." The way to find out if you've got something straight—if you've "perceived" it accurately—is to check it out, to ask if something meant what you think it did.

It takes courage because overseas you may feel stupid or embarrassed to do so. The challenge is to find a way to check your perceptions which does not make you feel uncomfortable and which is not offensive to your hosts.

One of the reasons we give all this attention to communication is because it is central to building cross-cultural relationships. And building relationships with host nationals is, in many respects, what it's all about.

Much of your effectiveness on the job and satisfaction in the overseas living experience with depend on how well you build working and social relationships with host nationals.

Skillful intercultural communication is a medium for finding out what expectations your hosts have of you and of getting across your expectations of them. It is a means of creating trust and communicating your sincerity and good will. It is a method of anticipating problems and solving those which arise. It is a channel for reaching out and establishing links with people.

18

Culture shock: Occupational hazard of overseas living

In preparing for the big move, you've probably had—or will soon have—all the vaccinations, innoculations and shots required. These will keep you safe from the dread diseases that can still be found in some parts of the world.

There is no vaccination, however, for one malady you are likely to encounter—culture shock. In all probability, the doctor who gave you your other shots wouldn't even have been able to talk intelligently about it.

"Culture Shock" is the term used to describe the more pronounced reactions to the psychological disorientation most people experience when they move for an extended period of time into a culture markedly different from their own. It can cause intense discomfort, often accompanied by hyper-irritability, bitterness, resentment, homesickness, and depression. In some cases distinct physical symptoms of psychosomatic illness occur.

For some people the bout with culture shock is brief and hardly noticeable. These are usually people whose personalities provide them with a kind of natural immunity. For most of us, however, culture shock is something we'll have to deal with over a period of at least several months, possibly a year or more.

In a sense, culture shock is the occupational hazard of overseas living through which one has to be willing to go in order to have the pleasures of experiencing other countries and cultures in depth.

All of us have known frustration at one time or another. Although related, and similar in emotional content, culture shock is different from frustration. Frustration is always traceable to a specific action or cause and goes away when the situation is remedied or the cause is removed. Some of the common causes of frustration are:

- the ambiguity of a particular situation
- the actual situation not matching preconceived ideas of what it would be like
- unrealistic goals
- not being able to see results
  —because of the enormity of the need
  —because of the nature of the work
  —because of the shortness of time of one's involvement
- using the wrong methods to achieve objectives (i.e., methods which are inappropriate to the new culture)

Frustration may be uncomfortable, but it is generally short-lived as compared to culture shock.

Culture shock has two quite distinctive features:

1. It does not result from a specific event or series of events. It comes instead from the experience of encountering ways of doing, organizing, perceiving or valuing things which are different from yours and which *threaten* your basic, unconscious belief that your enculturated customs, assumptions, values and behaviors are "right."

2. It does not strike suddenly or have a single principal cause. Instead it is cumulative. It builds up slowly, from a series of small events which are difficult to identify.

Culture shock comes from:

- being cut off from the cultural cues and known patterns with which you are familiar—especially the subtle, indirect ways you normally have of expressing feelings. All the nuances and shades of meaning that you understand instinctively and use to make your life comprehensible are suddenly taken from you.
- living and/or working over an extended period of time in a situation that is ambiguous.
- having your own values (which you had heretofore considered as absolutes) brought into question—which yanks your moral rug out from under you.

- being continually put into positions in which you are expected to function with maximum skill and speed but where the rules have not been adequately explained.

Regarding being cut off from your own cultural cues, Kalvero Oberg, the man who first diagnosed culture shock, says:

"These signs and clues include the thousand and one ways in which we orient ourselves to the situations of daily life: when to shake hands and what to say when we meet people, when and how to give tips, and how to give orders to servants, how to make purchases, when to accept and when to refuse invitations, when to take statements seriously and when not . . ."

These are just a few examples, but they show how *pervasive* is the disorientation out of which culture shock emerges.

THE PROGRESSIVE STAGES OF CULTURE SHOCK

As indicated above, culture shock progresses slowly. One's first reaction to different ways of doing things may be "How quaint!" When it becomes clear that the differences are not simply quaint, an effort is frequently made to dismiss them by pointing out the fundamental *sameness* of human nature. After all, people are really basically the same under the skin, aren't they?

Eventually, the focus shifts to the *differences* themselves, sometimes to such an extent that they seem to be overwhelming. The final stage comes when the differences are narrowed down to a few of the most troubling and then are blown up out of all proportion. (For Americans, standards of cleanliness, attitudes toward punctuality, and the value of human life tend to loom especially large.)

By now the sojourner is in an acute state of distress. The host culture has become the scapegoat for the natural difficulties inherent in the cross-cultural encounter. Culture shock has set in.

Here is a list of some of the symptoms that may be observed in relatively severe cases of culture shock.

- Homesickness
- Boredom
- Withdrawal (e.g., spending excessive amounts of time reading; only seeing other Americans; avoiding contact with host nationals)

- Need for excessive amounts of sleep
- Compulsive eating
- Compulsive drinking
- Irritability
- Exaggerated cleanliness
- Marital stress
- Family tension and conflict
- Chauvinistic excesses
- Stereotyping of host nationals
- Hostility toward host nationals
- Loss of ability to work effectively
- Unexplainable fits of weeping
- Physical ailments (psychosomatic illnesses)

Not everyone will experience this severe a case of culture shock, nor will all the symptoms be observed. Many people ride through culture shock with some ease, only now and again experiencing the more serious reactions. But many others don't. For them it is important to know 1) that the above responses can occur, 2) that culture shock is in some degree inevitable, and 3) that their reactions are emotional and not easily subject to rational management. This knowledge should give you a better understanding of what is happening to you and buttress your resolve to work at hastening your recovery.

Before we examine what you can do to counteract culture shock, let's spend a few minutes finding where it fits into the whole overseas experience.

Some time ago people began to recognize that there were distinct stages of personal adjustment which virtually everyone who lived abroad went through (no matter where they cam from or what country they were living in).

These stages are:

1. Initial euphoria
2. Irritability and hostility
3. Gradual adjustment
4. Adaptation or biculturalism.

1. Initial euphoria

Most people begin their new assignment with great expectations and positive mind-set. If anything, they come with expectations which are too high and attitudes that are too positive toward the host country and toward their own prospective experiences in it. At this point, anything new is intriguing and exciting. But, for the most part, it is the *similarities* which stand out. The recent arrivee is usually impressed with how people everywhere are really very much alike.

This period of euphoria may last from a week or two to a month, but the letdown is inevitable. You've reached the end of the first stage.

2. Irritation and hostility

Gradually, your focus turns from the similarities to the *differences*. And these differences, which suddenly seem to be everywhere, are troubling. You blow up little, seemingly insignificant difficulties into major catastrophes. This is the stage generally identified as "culture shock," and you may experience any of the symptoms listed on pages 65 and 66.

3. Gradual adjustment

The crisis is over and you are on your way to recovery. This step may come so gradually that, at first, you will be unaware it's even happening. Once you begin to orient yourself and to be able to interpret some of the subtle cultural clues and cues which passed by unnoticed earlier, the culture seems more familiar. You *become more comfortable in it* and feel less isolated from it.

Gradually, too, your sense of humor returns and you realize the situation is not hopeless after all.

4. Adaptation and biculturalism

Full recovery will result in an ability to *function in two cultures* with confidence. You will even find a great many customs, ways of doing and saying things, and personal attitudes which you enjoy—indeed, to which you have in some degree acculturated—and which you will definitely miss when you pack up and return home. In fact, you can expect to experience "reverse culture shock" upon your return to the U.S. (See

Postscript beginning on page 77.) In some cases, particularly where a person has adjusted exceptionally well to the host country, reverse culture shock may cause greater distress than the original culture shock.

The interesting thing about culture shock is that there are routinely not one but *two* low points and, even more interestingly, they will accommodate themselves to the amount of time you intend to spend in the host country! That is, they will spread themselves out if you're going to stay for a longer period or contract if your initial assignment is for a shorter time. You can't say that's not accommodating!

A graphic illustration of the "adjustment curve" can look something like that appearing below.

CULTURE SHOCK CYCLE
For A Two Year Assignment

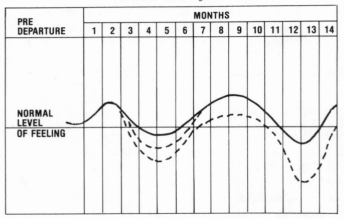

-----BROKEN LINES INDICATE THE EXTREME IN SEVERITY WITH WHICH CULTURE SHOCK MAY ATTACK.

How long will culture shock last?

As we have suggested, that varies with the length of your assignment. But it also depends to some extent on you and your resiliency. You can expect a let-up after the first dip, but be prepared for the second downturn which will probably be somewhat more severe.

Stop a moment and consider what you can do on you own to combat the onset and alleviate the effects of culture shock. What we have written so far in this book holds the key.

The next chapter offers our prescription.

19

Rx for culture shock

Granted that culture shock is virtually inevitable in some degree and that there are no easy remedies in the medicine cabinet, there are, nevertheless, things you can do. There are positive steps you can take to minimize the impact, and the sooner you take them, the better.

Here's our prescription for action:

1. Return to Chapter 13, "Know Thy Host Country" and *pursue your information gathering* assiduously. Go back to "Fifty Questions" and search out the answers you missed before. One of the best antidotes to culture shock—though when you're in the midst of it this may not make sense—is knowing as much as possible about where you are.

2. Begin (if you haven't been doing so already) consciously to *look for logical reasons* behind everything in the host culture which seems strange, difficult, confusing, or threatening. Even if your "reason" is wrong, it will reinforce the positive attitude that in fact there *is* a logical explanation behind the things you observe in the host culture. Take every aspect of your experience and look at it from the perspective of your hosts. Find patterns and interrelationships. All the pieces fit together once you discover where they go. Relax your grip on your own culture a little in the process. There's no way you can lose it (any more than you could forget to speak English), but letting go a bit may open up some unexpected avenues of understanding.

3. *Don't succumb to the temptation to disparage the host culture.* Resist making jokes and comments ("Well, what else would you expect from these people?") which are intended to illustrate the stupidity of the "natives," and don't hang around the Americans who do make them; they will only reinforce your unhappiness. Every post or American enclave has a number of people who have not been able to adjust to the country and who sit around waiting for the next boatload of American greenhorns to arrive so they can indoctrinate them on the "stupidity of the native." You see, they have high stakes in your discontent for, if they can get you to parrot back their gripes, it proves them right. Avoid these people like the plague! The sickness they are attempting to spread is far worse than any culture shock you will ever experience.

4. *Identify a host national* (a neighbor, someone at work, a friendly acquaintance) who is sympathetic and understanding, and talk with that person about specific situations and about your *feelings* related to them. Talking with Americans can be helpful but only to a limited extent (and not at all under certain circumstances—see the previous item on this list). Your problem lies in your relationship to the host culture.

5. Above all, have faith—in yourself, in the essential good will of your hosts, and in the positive outcome of the experience.

Indeed, you've probably got plenty going for you already. The next chapter will explore the attributes which experience has shown to be the most useful in adapting to a foreign environment.

20

Skills that
make a difference

Some people seem to take to another culture more naturally than others. And some foreign cultures seem to be easier for Americans to adjust to than others. But there are certain skills or traits which you may have—or, with a little effort, develop—which will facilitate your rapid adjustment.

Before going on, jot down in the space below some of the skills—they are usually attitudes, ways of responding, and styles of behaving—which you think might be most helpful in the overseas adjustment process.

NOTES:

Here are the skills which our experience has shown to be the most important:

- TOLERANCE FOR AMBIGUITY
- LOW GOAL/TASK ORIENTATION
- OPEN-MINDEDNESS
- NON-JUDGMENTALNESS
- EMPATHY
- COMMUNICATIVENESS
- FLEXIBILITY; ADAPTABILITY
- CURIOSITY
- SENSE OF HUMOR
- WARMTH IN HUMAN RELATIONSHIPS
- MOTIVATION
- SELF-RELIANCE
- STRONG SENSE OF SELF
- TOLERANCE FOR DIFFERENCES
- PERCEPTIVENESS
- ABILITY TO FAIL

Add to these any of yours which we did not list. Then on a scale of one (low) to five (high), rate yourself in each of these characteristics. Write the number beside each one and total them. If you scored less than 55 you've got some work to do.

Now circle the traits you think are the *most* important (or guess what our choices are—it'll be no surprise that we're going to tell you).

Our choices:

1. SENSE OF HUMOR
2. LOW GOAL/TASK ORIENTATION
3. ABILITY TO FAIL

A *sense of humor* is important because there is going to be much to weep or get angry or annoyed or embarrassed or discouraged about— no matter how many of the other traits you have, the ability to laugh things off will be the ultimate weapon against despair.

Americans abroad too often undertake *tasks* that are unrealistic and set *goals* for themselves that are unattainable. It is one of the major causes of failure. To the extent that you set your goals too high and refuse to adjust them to the realities of what can actually be accomplished in a foreign environment, you're going to be disappointed. Experience shows that Americans who are less goal-oriented or task-driven, and more able to relax and ride with events tend to be more effective and enjoy themselves overseas.

The ability to tolerate *failure* is critical because: 1) everyone fails at something overseas; it is absolutely built in, 2) the highest stars in the American firmament are "achievement" and "success," and 3) the American most likely to be selected to go overseas is the person who has been most successful at home. Some people sent abroad will have virtually never experienced failure. If, in addition, they have little tolerance for it, they are in for trouble as are those who work for or live with them.

One of the largest international cultural exchange organizations in the U.S.[13] uses "a sense of humor" and "the ability to fail" as principal selection criteria for the thousands of people they choose for international exchanges.

13. AFS International/Intercultural Programs

21

The challenge

We have called this book a "survival kit" because it deals with the personal pitfalls that await you overseas. We don't, by using the word "survival," envision you at the end of your tour abroad crawling on your hands and knees toward the plane, gaunt, unshaven, clothes in tatters, a hostile landscape behind you. On the contrary, we expect you survive the overseas experience very much on top.

But it probably won't be easy. Living in a foreign culture is like playing a game you've never played before and for which the rules haven't been explained very well. The challenge is to enjoy the game without missing too many plays, learning the rules and developing skills as you go along.

You'll learn a great deal, though much of it will be intangible and difficult to define. In negotiating the unfamiliar and uncharted territory of another culture, change and growth occur at deep levels, leaving you more competent, more self-assured and more knowledgeable about yourself and about how the world works.

BON VOYAGE!

22

Postscript:
So you're coming
back home?

Why does a book on overseas living have a chapter about coming back home? It's because the traveler needs to consider coming home as part of a complete cycle that includes leaving, settling overseas, and returning. And because it is sensible to prepare as diligently for re-entry as you did for the original exit and sojourn abroad. (Even so, don't be surprised if this chapter doesn't mean very much until re-entry draws near— at which time it should be re-read carefully.)

Just as the success of your overseas tour doesn't need to be left to luck, neither does your return home. The wise person plans ahead even when it's for coming back. You may reasonably wonder what you could possibly plan for beyond the bare logistics involved in the move. You know the language, the ways to get things done back home and, most likely, you will be returning to family, friends and a familiar setting. But these do not lessen your need to understand yourself better as an American who has been changed by the experience of living abroad and who will bring home a whole new load of cultural baggage. Further, during your absence changes have continued to take place in the U.S.— rapid and sometimes radical changes—and reading about them in *Time* or *Newsweek* isn't the same as experiencing them. You may think it will be easy to pick up where you left off; that's where the surprises come in.

In preparing for your return, it will be helpful to understand what re-entry shock is, the role your experiences overseas and the experience you missed in the U.S. play in it, and what you can do to counteract it.

WHAT IS RE-ENTRY SHOCK?

Some call it reverse culture shock. The curve on Page 70 is somewhat similar for re-entry, though the time frames will probably be different.

You'll recall we said the stages of the adjustment process are: 1. Initial euphoria; 2. Irritability and hostility; 3. Gradual adjustment; and 4. Adaptation.

In Stage 1, you may be very pleased, even euphoric, to be back in your own country, and others may be equally delighted to have you back. But after people express their pleasure at seeing you again, and listen politely to your stories for a few minutes, you may suddenly and/or painfully realize that they are not particularly interested in what happened to you abroad and would much prefer to talk about their own affairs. You may also find that the support system you encountered when you first arrived overseas—people who were willing and ready to help you settle into your new community—is not accessible back home. You are likely to find yourself completely on your own when it comes to buying a house or car or finding a job. People may help if you ask, but they're busy and you feel embarrassed about being so dependent—especially in your own country!

You may, therefore, find yourself entering Stage 2 more rapidly than you did overseas. Suddenly you find yourself irritated with others and impatient with your own inability to do things as well or as quickly as you had hoped.

While some people move readily on into the adjustment stage, others continue to feel alienated, even though they put on the outward appearance of doing well. Underneath, resentment, loneliness, disorientation, and even a sense of helplessness may pervade as the returnee experiences the kinds of culture shock symptoms identified on page 67 and 68. Depression, marital stress or, in children, regression to earlier stages of development may also be associated with re-entry shock.

The gap between you and your family and friends may be a source of significant irritation. So much that is different will have happened to you and to them that finding common ground will almost certainly be harder than expected.

You also will have learned new things: a foreign language, perhaps, or some local folk dances, or how to bargain in a market. But there's no outlet for them at home. Ways to use your skills can be found, but it takes effort and patience, and the frustrations tend to mount. You may feel let down because daily life in the U.S. doesn't readily provide the opportunity to meet as many kinds of people as you've known overseas. And the people you do meet seem very provincial and uninterested in things international.

America is also different. The pollution worse, the pace is more hurried and hectic, there is more violence on TV and more crime in the streets. In your job you may seem to have less authority and your work experience abroad may seem irrelevant or at least unappreciated by your colleagues and superiors.

Your status in general is lower, your standard of living goes down. You look like an American but you feel like a stranger. Your spouse feels lonely and out of place—at home! Your children are out of step with their classmates.

In short you will inevitably return from abroad bearing a whole host of expectations which, just as inevitably, will be disappointed, at least in some degree.

You will also have developed new attitudes, values and perceptions that are out of joint with what you find when you return. Here are some ways others have expressed their feelings:

"I see America through a sharper lens—both its strengths and its weaknesses. I no longer take this country for granted, and I really resent unbalanced criticism by Americans who don't know the rest of the world."

"I see the validity of at least one other culture. That makes me realize that the American way is not always right or best, and I am impatient with people whose blind acceptance of everything American causes them never to question anything."

"I have a less clear idea of 'home' now. Is it within myself or connected to my relationships, or is it linked to a certain place?"

"I don't understand some of the technological changes I see. So many people use personal computers. When I got back, I had my first experience in pumping gas into my car."

"I place more value on relationships than other Americans seem to. People here are too busy for one another."

"My oldest friend and I don't seem to have much to talk about any more. Her interests seem so 'shallow' to me now."

What can you do to counteract re-entry shock? In fact, the battle is mostly won when you understand that returning home involves an adjustment process similar to the one you experienced when first going abroad. Indeed, the practical steps we are going to recommend are quite similar to those we suggested for overseas adaptation:

1. Start your exploration of home through sympathetic friends or family members. Share with them some of the *feelings* you have had living overseas. Sharing feelings instead of experiences sounds less like bragging.

2. Find informants about the United States just as you did about your overseas country. Be the learner. Ask questions: What do you think about the current price of real estate? What are the good movies now? What was the Superbowl like? Where can I buy good produce? Any ideas on furniture sales? Where can I get help writing a resume? What do you think of present U.S. foreign policy?

In other words, play the foreigner. You really are in some ways. Learn your "new" culture just as you did your foreign culture. Don't let your new attitudes, values and *perceptions* (see chapter 17) prevent you from listening to and hearing what others are saying.

3. Ask a friend to make a list of new terms and fads to help you figure out what's going on in America. For instance:

New Vocabulary: (punk, new wave, valley girl, preppy)

New Technology: (Walkman, talking cars and elevators, computer games, cordless telephones, VTR's)

New Foods: (Potato skins, caffeine-free soft drinks, the new "American" cuisine)

What's "in": (gourmet foods, good manners, dressing well)

What's "out": (long hair for men, large American cars)

These examples may seem old by the time you read this but "new" ones will take their place.

4. Research various groups that may interest you: churches, schools, clubs, professional organizations, international and intercultural groups.

5. Explore places were you might find others with international experience or seek foreign nationals with whom you can speak the language(s) you've learned and continue to share common experiences you've enjoyed. (Most large and many small colleges and universities

have foreign students and scholars on campus, along with active international programs.) You may want to become a host to an exchange student or a visiting foreign family.

Sometimes we get trapped by our emotional responses and misjudge situations and the people around us. When a situation makes you feel uncomfortable, this simple three-step formula may help you deal with it:

First, *describe* (if only to yourself) the situation—what actually do you see happening?

Then, *interpret* what you see—what do you think about the situation?

Finally, *evaluate* those thoughts—what do you feel about the situation?

For example, let's say you have been invited to dinner by an American friend to celebrate your return. You're offered a well-prepared meal consisting of two courses: meat with vegetables and salad followed by dessert. But you have just come from a country where guests are offered at least three—sometimes four—courses, and salad is never served with hot dishes. You may find this meal disappointing.

1. *Describe:* This is a two course meal and the food is good.

2. *Interpret:* This is a customary American meal among friends and is not an expression of disdain for a guest.

3. *Evaluate:* I feel a little insulted (it doesn't seem "special" enough for the occasion) but when I get used to this custom, I probably won't react this way.

Now let's try it again with another scenario. You receive a phone call in the office from someone who knows you and hasn't seen you in a few weeks. He identifies himself and immediately makes a request. You have just come from a country where pleasantries are always exchanged before transacting business. It's really difficult for you to launch into a business discussion without first engaging in some social conversation. Using the describe/interpret/evaluation system, you may come up with something like this:

1. *Describe:* This person is calling for specific information.

2. *Interpret:* The purpose of this call is business and Americans tend to limit their social interaction during working hours.

3. *Evaluate:* I would rather re-establish personal contact before discussing business and feel like an object in this transaction. However, the caller's style doesn't imply a lack of regard for me as a person.

Or, to put it differently, these Americans have some peculiar customs, but they fit together in a logical pattern and are not intended to be offensive. American culture is just different, not wrong!

Remember that re-entry is a time when you can expect to go through a great deal of change and when you will be integrating those changes which have already occurred. It is completely normal to feel stressed during this time of adjustment, but just as you did abroad, you'll begin to feel "at home" again soon.

Appendices

THE KLUCKHOHN MODEL

ORIENTATION	RANGE		
	BASICALLY EVIL MUTABLE | IMMUTABLE	NEUTRAL | MIXTURE OF GOOD & EVIL MUTABLE | IMMUTABLE	BASICALLY GOOD MUTABLE | IMMUTABLE
HUMAN NATURE			
MAN-NATURE RELATIONSHIP	SUBJUGATION TO NATURE	HARMONY WITH NATURE	MASTERY OVER NATURE
TIME SENSE	PAST-ORIENTED (TRADITION BOUND)	PRESENT-ORIENTED (SITUATIONAL)	FUTURE-ORIENTED (GOAL-ORIENTED)
ACTIVITY	BEING (EXPRESSIVE/EMOTIONAL)	BEING-IN-BECOMING* (INNER DEVELOPMENT)	DOING (ACTION-ORIENTED)
SOCIAL RELATIONS	LINEALITY** (AUTHORITARIAN)	COLLATERALITY*** (COLLECTIVE DECISIONS)	INDIVIDUALISM**** (EQUAL RIGHTS)

EXPLANATIONS OF TERMS USED ABOVE:

*BEING-IN-BECOMING—THE PERSONALITY IS GIVEN TO CONTAINMENT AND CONTROL BY MEANS OF SUCH ACTIVITIES AS MEDITATION AND DETACHMENT, FOR THE PURPOSE OF THE DEVELOPMENT OF THE SELF AS A UNIFIED WHOLE.

**LINEALITY—LINES OF AUTHORITY CLEARLY ESTABLISHED AND DOMINANT-SUBORDINATE RELATIONSHIPS CLEARLY DEFINED AND RESPECTED; RIGHTS ACCORDING TO RANK.

***COLLATERALITY—MAN IS AN INDIVIDUAL AND ALSO A MEMBER OF MANY GROUPS AND SUB-GROUPS; HE IS INDEPENDENT AND DEPENDENT AT THE SAME TIME.

****INDIVIDUALISM—AUTONOMY OF THE INDIVIDUAL.

Source: Florence Kluckhohn and Fred Strodtbeck. *Variations in Value Orientations* (Evanston, Illinois: Row, Peterson & Co., 1961) (See especially Chapter 1.)

In terms of the VALUES they represent, the Kluckhohn Model would look like this:

ORIENTATION	RANGE		
HUMAN NATURE	MOST PEOPLE CAN'T BE TRUSTED.	THERE ARE BOTH EVIL PEOPLE AND GOOD PEOPLE IN THE WORLD, AND YOU HAVE TO CHECK PEOPLE OUT TO FIND OUT WHICH THEY ARE.	MOST PEOPLE ARE BASICALLY PRETTY GOOD AT HEART.
MAN-NATURE RELATIONSHIP	LIFE IS LARGELY DETERMINED BY EXTERNAL FORCES, SUCH AS GOD, FATE, OR GENETICS. A PERSON CAN'T SURPASS THE CONDITIONS LIFE HAS SET.	MAN SHOULD, IN EVERY WAY, LIVE IN COMPLETE HARMONY WITH NATURE.	MAN'S CHALLENGE IS TO CONQUER AND CONTROL NATURE. EVERYTHING FROM AIR CONDITIONING TO THE "GREEN REVOLUTION" HAS RESULTED FROM HAVING MET THIS CHALLENGE.
TIME SENSE	MAN SHOULD LEARN FROM HISTORY AND ATTEMPT TO EMULATE THE GLORIOUS AGES OF THE PAST.	THE PRESENT MOMENT IS EVERYTHING. LET'S MAKE THE MOST OF IT. DON'T WORRY ABOUT TOMORROW; ENJOY TODAY.	PLANNING AND GOAL-SETTING MAKE IT POSSIBLE FOR MAN TO ACCOMPLISH MIRACLES. A LITTLE SACRIFICE TODAY WILL BRING A BETTER TOMORROW.
ACTIVITY	IT'S ENOUGH TO JUST "BE." IT'S NOT NECESSARY TO ACCOMPLISH GREAT THINGS IN LIFE TO FEEL YOUR LIFE HAS BEEN WORTHWHILE.	MAN'S MAIN PURPOSE FOR BEING PLACED ON THIS EARTH IS FOR ONE'S OWN INNER DEVELOPMENT.	IF PEOPLE WORK HARD AND APPLY THEMSELVES FULLY, THEIR EFFORTS WILL BE REWARDED.
SOCIAL RELATIONS	SOME PEOPLE ARE BORN TO LEAD OTHERS. THERE ARE "LEADERS" AND THERE ARE "FOLLOWERS" IN THIS WORLD.	WHENEVER I HAVE A SERIOUS PROBLEM, I LIKE TO GET THE ADVICE OF MY FAMILY OR CLOSE FRIENDS IN HOW BEST TO SOLVE IT.	ALL PEOPLE SHOULD HAVE EQUAL RIGHTS, AND EACH SHOULD HAVE COMPLETE CONTROL OVER ONE'S OWN DESTINY.

APPENDIX B

A checklist for gathering basic factual information about your host country. These are the areas for which you will need to gather information. It is not essential, however, that you follow the exact sequence given here. If you're vitally interested in Section F, for example, start there.

A. **Symbols**
Symbolism of flag
National anthem
National flower, etc.

Myths and legends of
ethnic group(s)
National holidays
Traditional costumes

B. **Human and natural resources**
Geography and topography
Regional characteristics
Major cities
Natural resources (flora,
fauna, minerals)

Climate
Demographic information
Transportation systems
Communication systems
Mass communication media

C. **Family and social structure**
Family structure and
family life
Family roles
Social classes

Social organizations
Social welfare
Customs (re: birth, marriage,
death, etc.) and courtesies

D. **Religion and philosophy**
Religious beliefs (indigenous
and borrowed)

Proverbs
Superstitions

E. **Education**
   General approach (e.g., rote
   memorization vs. problem-
   solving approach)

   School system
   Colleges and universities
   Vocational training

F. **Fine arts and
   cultural achievements**
   Painting
   Sculpture
   Crafts
   Folk arts
   Architecture
   Music

   Dance
   Drama
   Literature
   Poetry
   Cinema

G. **Economics and industry**
   Principal industries
   Exports/imports
   Foreign investment
   Cottage industries (if any)
   Industrial development
   Modernization (if applicable)

   Urban and rural conditions
   Agriculture (crops and
   animal husbandry)
   Fishing (if it is a major
   activity)
   Marketing systems

H. **Politics and Government**
   System of Government
   Political parties
   Government organization
   (national and local)

   Current political figures
   Police system
   Military

I. **Science**
   Inventions and achievements
   (throughout history)

   Science
   Medicine

J. **Sports and games**
   Native sports (unique to
   the country)

   Modern world sports
   Traditional children's games

K. **National foods**

L. **National language**
   Local dialects/languages

APPENDIX C

A HUMAN PROFILE—QUESTIONS ABOUT SOCIAL PROCESSES, VALUES AND BEHAVIORS FOR THE "GRANDPARENTS' EXERCISE"

What would you teach your grandchildren about:

- Who they should obey?
- Who makes decisions (at home, in school, in the community)?
- How to behave with others (public officials, family members, neighbors, old people, other children, salespeople, etc.)?
- Who to respect and how to show respect for others?
- How they should act in public so they will be a credit to or bring honor upon their family?
- How important they are and can expect to be in the community?
- Who they should seek advice from when they need it?
- Who to trust?
- What it means to be successful in life?
- What the signs of success are?
- What provides "security?"
- How many children they should have?
- What is expected of children when they are young? when their parents are old?
- What to depend upon others for?
- When to be self-sufficient?
- What they can expose to others and what should be kept private or secret?
- How to plan for the future?
- What should be remembered from their heritage?
- What was better when you were young?
- What you wish for your grandchildren that you could not be or have?
- What it is they can depend upon as always being good or important?

- Why people work?
- What type of work they should prepare to do?
- Who their friends should be?
- Where they should live?
- Who they should marry and at about what age?

- What they should be wary or afraid of?
- How they can improve on what they are or have?
- *How* nature is beautiful?
- What they should be willing to sacrifice to insure a better life for more people?

APPENDIX D

CHECKLISTS OF LOGISTICS

The following lists are suggestive rather than exhaustive. You will probably add items which fit the particular country you are entering.

PREPARATIONS FOR ASSIGNMENT ABROAD[14]

Official documents

Apply for passport and any necessary visas. It is advisable to have separate passports for each family member. If the children are on the mother's passport, neither mother nor children can travel outside the country independently.

Doctors

Make appointments for medical examinations for each family member well in advance, three months ahead if possible, in order to be finished with series immunizations a month before departure date.

Request copies of any important records, x-rays, or prescriptions to go with you. Have prescriptions written in generic terms rather than with brand names.

Be sure to have each person's blood type in case a transfusion is needed.

Inquire about gamma globulin shots as a preventive measure against hepatitis.

Arrange to have copies of eyeglass prescriptions for any member of the family using glasses, as well as an extra pair of glasses for each.

Make dental appointments for each family member well in advance so all needed work can be completed by your dentist. Request instruc-

14. Prepared by SYSTRAN Corporation, used with permission.

tions on fluoride treatment abroad for children. Ask for copies of records, x-rays and statement of any recommended orthodontic treatment.

See your veterinarian for required shots and certificates if you are taking a pet with you. Write ahead to the United States Embassy in your country for current information on pet entry requirements. Consult with your veterinarian about preferred travel arrangements for your pet. Determine whether it will be necessary to inform someone abroad if the pet is to arrive in advance of the family.

Lawyer

Each adult member of the family should have an up-to-date will, properly witnessed and signed with the original placed in a safety deposit box, a copy for your lawyer, and a copy in your possession.

Draw up a power of attorney and leave it with a responsible relative or friend so that you have someone who can act legally in your behalf while you are abroad.

Bank

Arrange with your home bank to mail your monthly statements to you via airmail. If you have a safety deposit box with your home bank, arrange for copies of any papers you might need while overseas. Original naturalization papers can never be replaced so it is best to travel with copies only of these documents. Arrange power of attorney for someone within easy traveling distance of your bank to have access to your safety deposit box. The bank will need to register authorization and signature.

Obtain a supply of local currency for those countries to which you will be traveling to cover porters' tips, taxi fares, etc.

Purchase travelers' checks (preferably in small denominations) to cover hotel, restaurant, and sightseeing expenses while in route.

Put credit cards in safety deposit box until your return, except for the department store credit cards you will use for orders from abroad.

Schools

Notify your children's teachers of departure date in case special examinations must be scheduled to allow completion of term work. Request sufficient grade reports, test results, teacher evaluations, samples of work, etc. to facilitate grade placement in the new school.

Write schools in the new city for information or, if you are able to make a school selection prior to arrival, notify the school of your children's anticipated date of arrival, their grade level, and request space be held for them.

Insurance

Arrange for adequate insurance for your household effects and luggage. A floater policy will cover your belongings wherever they are, as well as injury to persons on your property or caused by a member of your household. Marine insurance for automobiles should be especially specified. If keeping your automobile insurance from this country, check to see if it covers your country of assignment. Some insurance companies abroad will give reduced rates if you produce a letter from your own company showing a no accident record.

Ascertain that you have appropriate health insurance coverage for your family. Even if full medical care is available with your company, coverage is desirable for home leave or emergency travel.

Post office

Complete a change of address card for your local post office. Obtain a supply of change of address cards to send to friends, Federal Income Tax Bureau, Department of Motor Vehicles, magazine subscriptions, etc.

Notify all charge accounts, magazine and newspaper subscriptions if you wish to terminate your account or to change your address.

Provide your family and friends with specific information on how to mail letters and packages to you. In some countries the duty will exceed the value of the package, so you may want to warn against sending gifts.

Department store

Pay a visit to a personal shopper at one or more of your favorite department stores in case you wish to order merchandise by mail from abroad. You will be registered and the process for your future orders will be clarified.

Check absentee voting procedure in case any special registration is required.

Obtain an international driver's license through the American Automobile Association (AAA).

Give notice of your moving date to all utility companies—gas, oil, water, electricity, telephone, etc. and discuss arrangements for billing and discontinuing service. Also notify the milkman, dry cleaners, and any other delivery service you may use.

Keep records of official expenses involved in the move.

IMPORTANT PAPERS TO ACCOMPANY YOU

On your person:

1. Passport
2. Shot records
3. Internationally recognized credit cards
4. U.S. and International driver's licenses (Plan to renew U.S. license by mail, if possible)

In your briefcase:

1. Copies of insurance policies
2. School records
3. Medical and dental records
4. Power of Attorney
5. Will
6. Inventories of personal luggage, air freight and household shipments
7. Extra passport photos
8. Record of your car motor and serial number

EMBASSY INFORMATION

Consular officials and their duties

The Chief of Mission with the title of Ambassador, Minister, or Charge d'Affairs, and the Deputy Chief of Mission are the heads of diplomatic missions. They are responsible for all parts of the mission within a country, including the consular post.

The Economic/Commercial Officers represent all the commercial interests in the country to which they are assigned. Their responsibilities include the promotion of trade and exports, arranging appointments for their citizens with local businessmen and government officials, and providing the maximum possible assistance to their country's businesses within the host country.

Political Officers study and report on local political developments and their possible effects on their country's interests.

Labor officers are well informed on labor in their particular countries and can supply information on wages, non-wage costs, local security regulations, etc.

The Consular Officers are the ones with whom you, as an expatriate, will have the most contact. Their function is to give you and your property the protection of your Government.

They maintain lists of their citizens living in the area, have lists of local attorneys, and act as liaison with police and other officials.

The Administrative Officer is in charge of the normal business operations of the post, including all purchasing for the Embassy or Consulate.

When you first arrive in your host country, register with the Embassy or Consulate nearest you. If there is an emergency, your relatives and friends will be able to locate you easily.

In addition, it will be useful to inquire about:[15]

Weather/climate conditions: What fabric in clothing wears longer, what special care personal and household items require.

Postal system: Dependability and efficiency of the postal system, location and appearance of post boxes, cost of mailing letters and packages.

Clothing sizes and availability: What will have to be imported, what clothing sizes translate into your size 14 dress or 9 shoe, the advisability of having clothes made.

Electricity: What voltage is used in the host country, can your appliances (including hair dryers) be adapted, which appliances are best left at home.

---

15. Excerpts from list prepared by Intercultural Network, Inc., used with permission.

Housing: Can arrangements be made prior to arrival; if not, where will you stay temporarily, how do you search for housing, what agreements with landlords are customary.

Furnishings and appliances: What "travels" well, how much shipping weight will you be allowed, when can shipped household items be expected to arrive, what is supplied in your new home (if you have acquired one).

Servants: Are servants available, how many will you need, how are they engaged, what are the customary wages and benefits offered by employers, what bonuses or special gifts are given, how are unsatisfactory servants dismissed.

Food restrictions (if any): What foods are unavailable, what are appropriate substitutes, what items will you want to import.

Health and hospitals: Where do you get emergency and other health care in country, what common maladies can you treat yourself and how.

Schools: Can your children attend public schools, what alternative schools are available, what are registration procedures, will uniforms be needed, is it necessary to place children in boarding schools at home.

Shopping: Who does the shopping, how often does one shop for food, what kind of stores for food and other necessities are available.

Baby-sitting arrangements: Who baby-sits, how is a sitter hired, what are the customary rates, are sitters "collected from" and returned home.

Laws and legal systems: What are the traffic laws, driving customs and conditions, obligations in case of an accident. We trust that you will not encounter the law in other instances but it is useful to know if there are any *unfamiliar* laws that you might break, literally by accident. For example, is it illegal to have liquor in your possession.

Employment possibilities for spouses: In most countries it is illegal to work without the proper permission. In many, those who accompany a spouse employed by a foreign firm are not permitted to work. It will be necessary to investigate various avenues to employment, if it is denied.

APPENDIX E

RESOURCES FOR FURTHER INFORMATION

1. **Country Studies** (formerly called "Area Handbooks") are available for 108 countries around the world. These excellent and informative books have been developed by the Foreign Area Studies Group at American University for the Department of Defense and other U.S. Government agencies. They are updated on a fairly regular basis and are available only from the Superintendent of Documents, U.S. Government Printing Office, Washington, D.C. 20402. Write for the list of countries covered.

2. **Country Updates** by Alison R. Lanier summarize the individual country data most important to the foreign traveler or resident. These *Updates* have been prepared for 19 countries and are the best available anywhere. They can be ordered through Intercultural Press, Inc., P.O. Box 768, Yarmouth, ME 04096.

3. Brief **"Culturegrams"** for 63 countries and the longer **Building Bridges of Understanding with the People of (country),** available for 11 countries, are published by the Language and Intercultural Research Center of Brigham Young University, 240/B-34, Provo, Utah 84602. Other useful materials on several countries are also published here.

4. **Background Notes** are very brief, factual information sheets developed by the U.S. Department of State and distributed by the Superintendent of Documents, U.S. Government Printing Office, Washington, D.C. 20402, for a minimal cost. They are available for 157 countries.

5. **Multinational Executive Travel Companion** is a useful but spotty publication that covers 160 countries. It is produced by Multinational Business Guides, World-Wide Business Centers, 575 Madison Avenue, Suite 1006, New York, NY 10022.

6. **Information Guide for Doing Business in (country)** is the basic title for a series of publications produced by Price Waterhouse and Co., 1251 Avenue of the Americas, New York, N.Y. 10020. So far, 48 countries are included.

7. **The Business Customs and Protocol** series has been produced for businessmen by the Stanford Research Institute. They concentrate on how to get started, how to get things done, and how to facilitate mutual understanding. They are available from S.R.I. International, 333 Ravenswood Avenue, Menlo Park, California 94025.

8. **International Business Travel and Relocation Directory,** Second Edition, Detroit: Gale Research Co., 1981. Gives information on business, travel and living conditions in the major world areas and the 40 countries which are most involved in world business activity.

9. **Global Guide to International Business** and **Global Guide to International Education,** by David S. Hoopes, New York: Facts on File Publications, 1984. The first title identifies resources for traveling, living and doing business overseas, broken down region by region and country by country. Also broken down region by region and country by country, the second title identifies resources for learning about other world areas and countries. Available through Intercultural Press, Inc., P.O. Box 768, Yarmouth, ME 04096.

10. **The Encyclopedia of the Third World** is published by Facts on File, 460 Park Avenue South, New York, New York 10016. There are three volumes in the series, sold only as a set, so you will probably want to check a library for this one.

11. **Interacts** is a relatively new series, so few books have been produced as yet, but it is a series to watch and wait for. They emphasize the cultural differences between Americans and nationals of a specific foreign country. Dealing with attitudes and concepts which are likely to give Americans trouble, they are published by the Intercultural Press, Inc., Box 768, Yarmouth, ME 04096.

12. **The World Today** series consists of six volumes covering Africa, Latin America, the Middle East and South Asia, the Far East and the Southwest Pacific, the Soviet Union and Eastern Europe, and Europe. You may purchase them, for a small amount, from Stryker-Post Publications, 888 17th Street, N.W., Washington, D.C. 20006.

13. **The Europa Yearbook** is published, in London, in two volumes. Also available are specialized volumes on Sub-Saharan Africa, the Middle East and North Africa. All are available from Gale Research Company, Book Tower, Detroit, Michigan, but again, this is one you will probably want to look up in your library.

14. **Cultures and People of the World** is an 11 volume set covering the 11 world areas. It is published and distributed by Pleasant Valley Press, Friends of History, Thorn Hill Industrial Park, 125 Commonwealth Drive, Warrendale, Pennsylvania 15086.

15. **Moving Abroad: A Guide to International Living,** by Virginia McKay, 1982. A handbook thoroughly covering the nitty-gritty details of moving overseas. Available from Intercultural Press, Inc.

16. **Traveler's Reading Guides,** edited by Maggy Simony, provide bibliographies for the world's countries in three volumes. Volume I covers Europe, Volume II, the Americas, and Volume III, the rest of the world. They are available at a reasonable price, from Freelance Publications, P.O. Box 8, Bayport, New York 11705.

17. **A Selected Functional and Country Bibliography For (region)** is the basic title for excellent bibliographies on the 8 major geographic regions of the world. They are updated regularly and available from The Center for Area and Country Studies of the Foreign Service Institute (U.S. Department of State), 1400 Key Boulevard, Arlington, Virginia 22209.

18. **Bibliographic Surveys** are annotated bibliographies prepared by the Department of the Army for certain areas of the world. Ten such volumes are available from the Superintendent of Documents, U.S. Government Printing Office, Washington, D.C. 20402.

19. **Human Relations Area File** (755 Prospect Street, New Haven, Conn. 06511) provides access to voluminous entries of an anthropological nature on all the cultures and subcultures of the world. The File includes much more than the casual reader would ever want to know but, for someone who wishes to delve more deeply, it is a gold mine. Copies of the File are housed in 20 universities around the United States.

20. Many American libraries now have access to computerized bibliographical banks which can, in short order and for minimal cost, produce an annotated bibliography on the country of your choice.

21. **How To Be a More Successful Language Learner,** by Joan Rubin and Irene Thompson, Boston: Heinle and Heinle (Also available from the Intercultural Press, Inc.). This is a practical guide describing techniques for making language learning easier and more efficient.